*The Origins of the Cold War*

# The Origins
# of the
# Cold War

## Lloyd C. Gardner
*Rutgers, The State University of New Jersey*

## Arthur Schlesinger, Jr.
*The City University of New York*

## Hans J. Morgenthau
*The City University of New York*

*Ginn and Company*
*A Xerox Company*

*Waltham, Massachusetts | Toronto*

*The American Forum Series*

CONSULTING EDITORS

J. Joseph Huthmacher
*University of Delaware*

Warren I. Susman
*Rutgers, The State University of New Jersey*

# Editors' Introduction

For more than a generation the Cold War has been a central influence in the lives of Americans; it is not surprising, therefore, that interest in tracing the origins of that pervasive phenomenon runs high among the nation's historians and students. But, as in the case of most efforts to probe the causes of profound historical developments, explanations of the origins of the Cold War have become more subtle and complex, rather than simpler, with the passage of time.

At the outset, during the Truman years, most Americans and most American historians accepted the "official" interpretation of the Cold War developed by the administration in power to explain and justify its foreign policies. According to this version,

America's wartime vision of a peaceful and progressive postwar world, built upon principles of collective security sustained by the United Nations and continuing Big Power collaboration, was shattered by the resurfacing of Russian ambitions to foment revolution and conquest on behalf of communism's cause. The United States' political, economic, and military responses to this threat represented her assumption of leadership among the "peace-loving" peoples of the world in defense of self-determination and other "democratic" values.

A few political figures at the time rejected the "Liberal Establishment" interpretation of the Cold War—Henry Wallace is one example—but Wallace's poor showing as an independent candidate for the Presidency in 1948 indicated how little popular support his position commanded. A larger number among the nation's intellectuals also refused to assign the "blame" for the Cold War exclusively to Communist Russia; see, for example, Walter Lippmann's *The Cold War* (New York: Harper and Brothers), published in 1947. But for the most part, the country's historians praised Truman as a "realist" in foreign affairs, and a poll of social scientists conducted by Professor Arthur Schlesinger, Sr. as late as 1962 ranked the Missourian high among the "near great" occupants of the White House. Textbooks of the period commonly conveyed the anti-Communist interpretation of the Cold War to thousands of students, as did books so widely used in the nation's classrooms as Arthur Schlesinger, Jr.'s *The Vital Center* (Boston: Houghton Mifflin, 1949), George F. Kennan's *American Diplomacy, 1900–1950* (New York: New American Library, 1951), and Eric F. Goldman's *The Crucial Decade* (New York: Knopf, 1956).

During the 1950's the Cold War assumed new forms and expanded into additional areas of the world. Despite the Eisenhower administration's early attacks on Truman's "containment" policies (see John Foster Dulles, "A Policy of Boldness," *Life*, XXXII [May 19, 1952], pp. 146ff), the Republican regime continued to apply Truman's basic policies in practice. The administration, and the majority of the American people, continued to adhere to the official explanation of the Cold War's origins and nature that had evolved during the Truman years (see John W. Spanier, *American Foreign Policy since World War II* [New York: Praeger, 1960]).

Nevertheless, during the 1950's various forms of "revisionism" also made headway among historians of the Cold War. A growing number of them adopted the view, suggested even earlier by Hans J. Morgenthau and a few others, that postwar Moscow-directed challenges to American interests in Europe represented manifestations of specifically *Russian*, rather than *Communist*, ambitions. The Cold War had originated as a relatively narrowly limited affair, therefore. The United States should not make the mistake of escalating it to global proportions, for America could not realistically undertake to play "policeman to the world."

Much more radically revisionist was the position that held the United States, rather than either Russia or communism, responsible for beginning the Cold War. Under the leadership of Professor William Appleman Williams, the so-called "Wisconsin School" of diplomatic historians portrayed American foreign policy as essentially a function of the nation's capitalist socioeconomic system. Since at least the late nineteenth century, according to this interpretation, American policy consistently aimed at creating an international polity that would be most conducive to American business expansion and commercial penetration. To those among the emerging "New Left" who pushed the Williams thesis to its most extreme implications, the Cold War thus represented only the latest and most ambitious outburst of American economic imperialism—an imperialism reinforced now with the power of nuclear weaponry. See William Appleman Williams, *The Tragedy of American Diplomacy* (Cleveland: World Publishing Company, 1959), D. F. Fleming, *The Cold War and Its Origins* (London: Allen & Unwin, 1961), David Horowitz, *The Free World Colossus* (New York: Hill and Wang, 1965), Gar Alperovitz, *Atomic Diplomacy: Hiroshima and Potsdam* (New York: Simon & Schuster, 1965), the several essays on foreign affairs in Barton J. Bernstein (ed.), *Towards a New Past* (New York: Pantheon, 1968), and Gabriel Kolko, *The Politics of War: The World and United States Foreign Policy, 1943–1945* (New York: Random House, 1968).

As criticism of America's role in Vietnam and elsewhere mounted during the 1960's, the New Left's simplistic *anti*-American view of the origins of the Cold War gained popularity particularly among the younger generation of Americans, even as many of their elders held tenaciously to the simplistic *pro*-American interpretation they had imbibed during their formative years. Among scholars of the Cold War, however, there developed a noticeable tendency away from simplistic views, and toward a subtle blending of the hypotheses that had gone before. Writers like Louis Halle (*The Cold War as History* [London: Chatto & Windus, 1967]) and Walter LaFeber (*America, Russia, and the Cold War* [New York: John Wiley and Sons, 1967]) seemed able to take a more dispassionate view, approaching the post-World War II developments that gave rise to the Cold War with much the same detachment they might bring to a study of diplomatic settlements in post-Napoleonic Europe. In such treatments the assignment of "blame" for the Cold War is of minor concern; instead, the study of the Cold War's origins becomes simply part of the long chronicle of misplaced fears, inevitable frustrations, and mutual foibles that make up the history of international relations and, indeed, of mankind. Even though this degree of "objectivity" has recently been attained, however, one cannot be certain that the argument over the Cold War's origins has been exhausted or definitively settled, even on the scholarly level. For one thing, all of the records bearing on the subject have not yet been examined. At this writing former President Truman still has in his personal possession documents from his administration which some authorities believe may shed new light on important aspects of post-World War II American–Russian relations; other documents in American depositories are shrouded in secrecy; and no American scholar has yet been granted access to Moscow's archives. Moreover, who can tell what effects another shift in the external world situation—which has governed attitudes toward the Cold War so importantly in the past—may produce upon the writing of Cold War history in the future?

In any event, the essays and rejoinders by three distinguished authorities presented in this volume, written from varying points of view, are representative of the most recent scholarly analysis of the origins of the Cold War, and to a considerable extent they also reflect the main trends in the historiography of the Cold War just summarized. Each of the essays is rooted in one of the "schools" of interpretation referred to earlier, yet they are characterized by the refinement and sophistication which those interpretations have acquired with the passage of time. Each of the rejoinders was written especially for The American Forum Series, and reflects the writer's response to the essays by his fellow participants. Significant differences still exist, for example, between Arthur Schlesinger, Jr., often considered a spokesman for the Liberal Establishment, and Lloyd C. Gardner, a member of the "Wisconsin School," yet their differences are not argued in the simplistic terms that most likely would have obtained in an earlier time. Some may conclude that the general movement seems to be away from extreme polarization of attitudes and toward some middle point, represented in this collection perhaps to some extent by the position taken by Hans Morgenthau. If so, are historians merely mirroring the trend in the external world situation, in years when a notable thaw seems to have taken place in American–Russian relations?

Notwithstanding that the ardor of the argument over the origins of the Cold War may have subsided somewhat, more than enough questions stimulative to reflection and debate should occur to the reader as he digests these essays. Some of them are endemic to any inquiry of the kind undertaken here. For example, when we seek out the "origin" of an epochal historical development, are we searching for a paramount specific event, or are we dealing with an intricate web of interrelated phenomena over an extended period of time? Of the various kinds of causative factors definable —political, military, ideological, economic, cultural, and the rest— which is *the* most important; or is such a question in itself irrelevant and misleading? Is it a legitimate part of the scholar's task to assign or apportion "blame" in the course of analyzing events that have had direful results for society?

The reader may wish to test the authors who are included in this volume in terms of the degree to which, consciously, or unconsciously, they touch upon such matters in the writings. In addition, another order of questions will arise from the substantive content of the essays as each of them explores the specific historical problem of the origins of the Cold War. To what extent is Professor Gardner justified in his assignment of a continuity to American foreign policy throughout the twentieth century; or Professor Morgenthau in his assignment of a continuity to Russian foreign policy under both the Czars and the Communists? How does Professor Schlesinger's emphasis on Stalin's personality affect his assessment of the role that ideology has played in the Cold War? All three of the authors allude to the trait of "universalism" as an important factor in the traditional world outlook of Americans. But how does each author define this trait? Does he consider it a positive or negative factor? If the latter, what does he explicitly or implicitly propose as a desirable alternative to "universalism"?

The comparative approach to the study of the origins of the Cold War which this book presents, then, should provide an exercise both in the more general problems associated with the study of causation in history, and in the substantive study of an important aspect of the recent American past. But more than that, the comparative approach should prove relevant and useful for the consideration of present and future action in the field of public policy. For while the Cold War may now be history—and dead—as some have proclaimed, America's role as a major world power is not likely to diminish substantially for some time to come. Study of the Cold War's origins, and of America's relationship thereto, may be instructive in terms of international dilemmas that still lie ahead. It may even help us to avoid some of the kinds of mistakes that have been made in the past.

J. JOSEPH HUTHMACHER
WARREN I. SUSMAN

# A Chronology of Early Cold War Events 1945–1949

| | |
|---|---|
| February 4–11, 1945 | Yalta Conference. |
| April 12, 1945 | Death of President Franklin D. Roosevelt. |
| April 23, 1945 | White House Meeting of Truman and Molotov. |
| April 25, 1945 | UN Conference opens in San Francisco. |
| May 8, 1945 | V-E Day. |
| May 25, 1945 | Harry Hopkins arrives in Moscow. |
| July 5, 1945 | Polish Government recognized by Western powers. |
| July 16, 1945 | Successful Atomic Test at Alamogordo, New Mexico. |
| July 17, 1945 | Potsdam Conference opens. |

| | |
|---|---|
| August 6, 1945 | Bombing of Hiroshima. |
| August 8, 1945 | Russia declares war on Japan. |
| August 9, 1945 | Bombing of Nagasaki. |
| August 14, 1945 | V-J Day. |
| August 18, 1945 | Secretary of State Byrnes attacks rigging of elections in Bulgaria. |
| September 1945 | Council of Foreign Ministers Meeting in London. |
| December 1945 | Council of Foreign Ministers Meeting in Moscow. |
| March 5, 1946 | Churchill's Iron Curtain Speech in Fulton, Missouri. |
| May 1946 | Russia leaves Iran after pressure from UN. |
| October 1946 | Peace treaties for Nazi satellites agreed upon. |
| March 10, 1947 | Moscow Conference of Foreign Secretaries. |
| March 12, 1947 | Truman Doctrine Speech. |
| March–August, 1947 | Communists smash ruling party in Hungary. |
| June 5, 1947 | Marshall Plan announced. |
| August 2, 1947 | Marshall Plan rejected by Russia. |
| October 5, 1947 | Formation of Cominform. |
| February 25, 1948 | Czech *coup*. |
| June 1948 | Cominform expels Yugoslavia. |
| June 1948–May 1949 | Berlin Blockade. |
| March–August 1949 | Formation of NATO. |

# Contents

*The Origins of the Cold War*

# Essays

# 1

# Lloyd C. Gardner

*Born in Delaware, Ohio in 1934, Lloyd C. Gardner studied at Ohio Wesleyan University and took his Ph.D. at the University of Wisconsin. Currently Professor of History at Rutgers, the State University of New Jersey, Mr.* Gardner has published Economic Aspects of New Deal Diplomacy *(Madison: University of Wisconsin Press, 1964) and* Architects of Illusion: Men and Ideas in American Foreign Policy, 1941–1949 *(Chicago: Quadrangle, 1970), and has edited* A Different Frontier: Selected Readings in the Foundations of American Economic Expansion *(Chicago: Quadrangle, 1966).*

*The present essay was written by Mr. Gardner especially for The American Forum Series.*

**I**n the ruin and smoking rubble that was Berlin in May 1945, two converging lines at last intersected. Rapidly spreading outward from this fateful conjunction in both time and space arose the "Cold War." Behind the meeting of these lines were the pressures of nearly three decades of ideological conflict between the Soviet Union and the capitalist powers. Temporarily submerged under the precarious weight of official press handouts extolling the Grand Alliance, some "contradictions" began to show through the rhetoric as the war in Europe neared its end. Fully aware of such tensions, Hitler's desperate successors sought to exploit the "Red Peril" to save the moribund Nazi leadership in the bunkers beneath Berlin.  On April 28, 1945, the British Broadcasting Corporation monitored the following appeal:

> If Berlin falls, Europe will fall with it. . . . In these critical days the Fuehrer has taken the major decision that, whatever else happens, the available strength of the Reich shall be concentrated on the attempt to prevent the Bolshevik flood from rolling westwards. This is not merely a German but a European decision. . . . It is indeed a ghastly and obscene irony that the men who are defending the Western world against the mighty hordes from hither Asia should be stabbed in the back by the Western democracies.

Eight days before that radio broadcast was picked up in London, the American Ambassador to the Soviet Union informed President Harry S. Truman of his opinion that "we" were faced with a "barbarian invasion of Europe." Juxtaposing these statements quite obviously exaggerates the immediate reaction to the "Red Peril," but even if it did not save the Third Reich from its fate, the Germans had the right idea: the Western victors were haunted by the spectre of the Red Army marching into the chaos of Central Europe, and spreading farther west through avenues prepared by internal subversion and political anarchy.

But there were other dimensions to the emerging Russian-American confrontation. Even before the Bolshevik Revolution—in fact twenty years before that upheaval—the United States and Imperial Russia had edged close to a major conflict on the Asian mainland, a conflict characterized by the similarities of each nation's development in the last decade of the nineteenth century, and by the even more striking differences in their economic and political methods. Each had pushed towards the Orient in the final thrust of world capitalism and European imperialism before World War I. Eastward from European Russia stretched the tracks of the Trans-Siberian Railway. Its backers counted on its bringing back enough of Asia's treasure to redeem their promises —and mortgage notes. In a similar quest, the sponsors of America's great transcontinental railroads laid plans for spanning the Pacific Ocean. As they did, policymakers in Washington decided upon war with Spain. In a few months' time the United States became an Asian power to be reckoned with by all nations.

From its new outpost in the Philippines, Washington sent armed forces to take part in the suppression of the Boxer Rebellion. At the conclusion of these efforts, Secretary of State John Hay asked the powers to join the United States in guaranteeing the territorial integrity of China and in assuring equality of opportunity for all nations in the China trade. Clutching Manchuria tenaciously, imperial Russia put off all American challenges with diplomatic evasions.

Before this prospective contest for supremacy in Manchuria and China could reach the point of a showdown, if indeed it ever would have, came the dramatic Japanese attack in 1904 upon the Russian fleet harbored at Port Arthur. Though aware of possible future dangers to United States interests in a Japanese victory, President Theodore Roosevelt was delighted at this blow to Russian aspirations. He was fully convinced, as he said upon occasion, that Japan was "playing our game." But at the end of World War II there was no one who could play the hand by proxy. When the guns stopped firing, American military units faced the Red Army across battle lines in both Europe and Asia.

In most of these places the confrontation quickly froze into "Cold War" situations. At the time of the Berlin Blockade by the Soviets in 1948, the United States very nearly decided to send tanks across the Autobahn to test Russian willingness to face a military showdown; in 1950 the United States took part in the Korean War rather than risk seeming unwilling to face a similar challenge. Behind Washington's military viceroys in these places was the awesome power of the atomic bomb. The bomb made it possible to take more risks, on the other hand, in dealing with Soviet-American political and economic conflicts, some of which, at least, had not changed substantively in the fifty years from 1895 to 1945. The United States still sought to extend the principle of the Open Door, "a fair field and no favor"; the Russians still pursued their goals by authoritarian methods behind iron curtains.

With the conclusion of a second world war within that fifty-year period, however, responsibility for restoration of the capitalist world order fell to the United States. American leaders had been granted a "second chance," as Professor Robert Divine said recently; a second chance to assume the political responsibilities the nation had turned away from at the end of World War I, a second chance also to construct an economic order more progressive and more lasting than the British century after Waterloo. There was not likely to be a third chance.

"The fact is," Henry Luce had written in that remarkable little book, *The American Century*, in 1941, "that Franklin Roosevelt failed to work successfully on a narrow, materialistic basis. . . . Our only chance now to make it work is in terms of a vital international economy and in terms of an international moral order." Luce's gloomy assessment of the 1930's was not shared by all American leaders, but most were deeply troubled about the shape of the postwar world, and believed that the only chance for American democracy was in the kind of world the publisher described.

Their greatest fear was that Stalin would exploit the political appeal of "leftist" movements, creating conflicts within nations which, unless checked by the forces of social order, would very probably lead to a conflict between the United States and the Soviet Union. "Unless they are absolutely out of their minds," Dean Acheson remarked privately in 1947, "the Politburo will carefully avoid war. . . . They will move in through international brigades as they had used in Hungary." [1]

The Soviet Union, then, presented a bifurcated challenge to the first generation leaders of the American century in 1945: the physical presence of the Red Army in Eastern Europe diminished the chances for European recovery from the effects of the war, while the spiritual presence of Kremlin-directed Communist activity threatened world stability. Ironically, America's strongest

---

[1] Quoted in David Lilienthal, *The Journals of David Lilienthal*, 2 vols. (New York: Harper & Row, 1964), *II*, pp. 213–15.

ally again such "adventurism" was probably Stalin himself. Having abandoned Greek Communists to a British fate in 1944, a few months later he advised Mao Tse-tung's representatives to go home and work somehow within the oppressive and corrupt Kuomintang. "So little did Stalin think of turning the Cominform into any genuine instrument of international revolution," observed Isaac Deutscher, "that he did not ask the Chinese and other Asian parties to join the new organization." [2] Of course, much of this was unknown at the time, and much more was badly misinterpreted. Moreover, though Stalin exercised almost total power inside Russia, he could not control events even within the world Communist movement as later occurrences in both Yugoslavia and China well demonstrated.

What would happen, asked Secretary of Defense James V. Forrestal during the summer of 1947, if Russia issued a *démarche* and France and Italy went Communist as a result? President Harry S. Truman replied that then "we" would have to look to history for our answer, to Rome and Carthage, to Athens and Sparta, to Alexander and the Persians, to France and England, to England and Germany.[3] In these analogies, as in other statements by American leaders, the Russian challenge became blurred into a general menace capable of being turned into a justification for almost any response—even preventive war. Though there were some Cold War leaders who pleaded with the Administration to maintain its poise and perspective, their voices grew fainter and finally disappeared in the hysteria of the arms race and McCarthyism.

But no American leader ever seriously maintained that preventive war was the solution to the Russian/Communist challenge. "We can't stand another global war," President Truman told a Missouri audience on October 7, 1945. "We can't ever have another war, unless it is a total war, and that means the end of our civilization as we know it. We are not going to do that. We are

---

[2] Isaac Deutscher, *Stalin: A Political Biography*, 2nd ed. (New York: Oxford University Press, 1967), p. 586.
[3] Walter Millis (ed.), *The Forrestal Diaries* (New York: Viking Press, 1951), p. 281.

going to accept the 'golden rule' and we are going forward to meet our destiny which I think Almighty God intended us to have. *And we are going to be the leaders*." [4]

What Truman meant by being the "leaders" defined the American position in the Cold War, and was nowhere more clearly set forth than by Secretary Forrestal during 1947:

> As long as we can outproduce the world, can control the sea and can strike inland with the atomic bomb, we can assume certain risks otherwise unacceptable in an effort to restore world trade, to restore the balance of power—military power—and to eliminate some of the conditions which breed war.[5]

Stalin's postwar goals for what Deutscher aptly calls "socialism in one sphere," were detailed in his February 9, 1946 "election" in which he called for "three or more five-year plans." Some western observers professed to see in this a veiled appeal, Leninist-style, to the underdeveloped nations of the world to adopt Communist development schemes in preference to backward capitalist methods. Others were far more interested in that part of the speech where Stalin told the Russian people that "our Marxists" had warned him that a new struggle within the capitalist world was inevitable, and that it endangered the Soviet Union. Several prominent Americans interpreted this statement to mean that he was really preparing his nation for a struggle with the West. Justice William O. Douglas, for example, suggested that it amounted to a declaration of World War III—Stalin would fill in the date when he was ready.

The pattern of events following the German surrender until Truman stood before Congress in March 1947 to ask for aid in the world struggle with communism—then virulent in Greece and Turkey—seemed inevitable to many of the participants, who wrote their memoirs and provided historians with their views and

---

[4] Department of State, *Bulletin, XIII* (October 14, 1945), 557–58.
[5] Walter Millis (ed.), *The Forrestal Diaries* (New York: Viking Press, 1951), pp. 350–51.

their selection of the pertinent facts. Soon these specific recollections were gathered together in the collective memoirs which made up the first histories of the Cold War.

It is now clear that major weaknesses existed in the original interpretation, and its reexamination has revealed several old questions that were never really answered by it, as well as additional ones to be confronted now.

## Roosevelt's Dilemma, or, the Perils of Second Front Diplomacy

When Nazi Germany turned on its strange ally, Soviet Russia, in the summer of 1941, Prime Minister Winston Churchill immediately sent envoys to Moscow to work out the necessary political aspects of their unexpected military alliance. Without any assurance that America would come into the European war, or that when it finally did come in there would still be a chance to save British interests, Churchill was faced with grim alternatives. Even if Germany defeated Russia, anything he could do to prolong Stalin's resistance might give him the margin of victory. He was in a weak position to resist Soviet demands for its Nazi Pact frontiers.

Awareness of British desperation, coupled with a growing sense that sooner or later the United States would be in the shooting war, made official Washington alert to the despatch of this mission, and wary of its outcome. American military observers thought it would be unwise to recognize any of its results since Stalin would soon give up the fight, and attempt to make good his claims after the war was settled in the West. Senator Harry Truman had a thought which appealed to many, at least emotionally: Aid whichever side, Russia or Germany, that seemed to be winning at the moment until both were exhausted, provided Hitler did not somehow emerge victorious.

What Roosevelt did in this instance was to urge Great Britain to make a public statement affirming that "no postwar peace commitments as to territories, populations, or economics have been given." [6] He would then issue a supporting statement in Washington. This message initiated the correspondence leading to the Atlantic Conference of Roosevelt and Churchill in August 1941, at the conclusion of which a joint statement given out by the two political leaders was quickly headlined as the "Atlantic Charter."

Upon returning to England, the Prime Minister was met with embarrassing questions concerning the Atlantic Charter's promises of self-determination and other pledges so reminiscent of Wilson's "Fourteen Points." What did the Charter mean for the future of the Empire, particularly its Far Eastern possessions? The Prime Minister finally replied to these queries on the floor of the House of Commons. The pronouncement, he declared, did not apply to internal affairs of the Empire. Privately he confided to aides that he had also rejected a strong attempt to write in America's postwar economic program as an integral part of the Charter itself. He had thereby protected the British imperial preference trade system.

The importance of mentioning these public and private reservations by the British government becomes apparent when it is noted that the Soviet government adhered to the Atlantic Charter a short time after—*but with its own reservations:* "Considering that the practical application of these principles will necessarily adapt itself to the circumstances, needs, and historic peculiarities of particular countries, the Soviet government can state that a consistent application of these principles will secure the most energetic support on the part of the government and peoples of the Soviet Union." [7]

That response was not unlike the Czar's answer to Secretary Hay's Open Door notes on China in 1899 and 1900; and Hay's counterresponse at the time was still typical of American policy in 1941: Ignore the reservations and give the widest possible cir-

---

[6] Department of State, *Foreign Relations of the United States, 1941* (Washington, D.C.: Government Printing Office), *I*, p. 342.

[7] This important caveat was recently called to everyone's attention for the first time by Martin F. Herz, *Beginnings of the Cold War* (Bloomington, Indiana: Indiana University Press, 1966), pp. vii–viii.

culation to the general acceptance of the "principle." This stance
covered up serious differences among the new allies, and presumed
too much, far too much, for the ultimate effectiveness of American economic and moral power. Actually it was British policy
in India which called forth the first attempted exercise of that
moral power, of "pitiless publicity," as Roosevelt once called it.
On Washington's Birthday 1942 the President responded to domestic criticisms that he was in complicity with British efforts to
deny India its independence with the following generalization:
"The Atlantic Charter applies not only to the parts of the world
that border on the Atlantic but to the whole world. . . ." [8]

Roosevelt's public lecture to the British followed by several
weeks his private intervention in Anglo-Russian negotiations.
Churchill had resisted Stalin's persistent and increasingly threatening territorial demands since the midsummer conference in Moscow. In early November another message came from Stalin
insisting upon some settlement of the political affairs at issue as
well as definite understandings on the military side of the Anglo-
Russian effort against Hitler. Once again Anthony Eden was sent
to Moscow. Despite the moral support of the Atlantic Charter
and more tangible American aid from Lend-Lease, the British
position was little stronger than it had been. Just before the British
Foreign Minister left, the American Ambassador brought to the
Foreign Office a cable from Washington which concluded with a
stiff warning: "Above all there must be no secret accords." It
was dated December 5, 1941—two days *before* Pearl Harbor.

When Eden replied to Russian demands by referring to the
Atlantic Charter and His Majesty's Government's commitment
to the United States position that territorial settlements must
await the postwar peace conferences, Stalin exploded dramatically. He said that he was "genuinely surprised" that this should
be the case. "I thought that the Atlantic Charter was directed
against those . . . who were trying to establish world dominion.

---

[8] Robert E. Sherwood, *Roosevelt and Hopkins: An Intimate History* (New
York: Harper, 1950), p. 507.

It now looks as if the Charter was directed against the U.S.S.R." [9]

This crisis passed when Eden promised to present the Russian arguments to the War Cabinet, and assured him that the matter would be settled before the Red Army could recapture the areas in question. A third round of talks on political issues in Eastern Europe began in London the following March. Churchill did not have the military power either to relieve the Russian front, or to make Stalin respect British wishes politically. He was inclined at this point to concede the Baltic countries and Poland. But he could not do it alone. "The principles of the Atlantic Charter," he advised Roosevelt, "ought not to be construed so as to deny to Russia the frontiers which she occupied when Germany attacked her." [10]

The State Department had been expecting something along these lines over the wires from London for several days. After discussing the possibility that the British were overly frightened by one of Stalin's recent speeches which could have been interpreted as a threat to make a separate peace if these demands were not soon satisfied, department officers urged that no concessions be made. Their feeling about the matter was, noted one participant, "if we make a single commitment regarding the peace we have lost the chance of being free agents." [11]

A former ambassador to the Soviet Union, William C. Bullitt, also urged the President directly to demand pledges from Stalin—thus reversing the diplomatic initiative (and pressure)—otherwise, "the vital interests of the American people covered by our Atlantic Doctrine [the Atlantic Charter] and our Open Door doctrine . . ." would be imperiled by one "vast dictatorship from the Pacific

---

[9] See William L. Neumann, *After Victory: Churchill, Roosevelt, Stalin and the Making of the Peace* (New York: Oxford University Press, 1967), pp. 50–51; all the key documents are in State Department, *FR, 1942, III*, pp. 491–524.

[10] E. L. Woodward, *British Foreign Policy in the Second World War* (London: Her Majesty's Stationery Office, 1962), p. 193.

[11] "Notes on a Visit to Washington," March 2, 3, 4, 1942: in *The Papers of J. Pierrepont Moffat*, Houghton Library, Harvard University, Cambridge, Massachusetts.

to Western Europe." [12] Less dogmatic than the State Department, Roosevelt tested several ways of meeting the Soviet challenge before settling upon "Second Front Diplomacy."

Asking Stalin to send Molotov to Washington, the President first offered to expand the Atlantic Charter partnership into the joint operation he now called the Big Four. He suggested to the Russian diplomat that Premier Stalin should participate fully in formulating a trust program for "many islands and colonial possessions which ought, for our own safety, to be taken away from weak nations." [13]

No Western statesman had ever spoken to a Bolshevik in such intimate terms, but far from erasing the leftover suspicions from the prewar ideological conflict, this proposal probably only puzzled Molotov and the Kremlin. Why that should be so can be explained in a few paragraphs and it illustrates some of Roosevelt's problems as a war leader.

The Big Four was a creation of Roosevelt's imagination. It reduced postwar thinking, serious postwar thinking, to the level of a Western sheriff handing out badges to his deputies. Despite American hopes and dreams since 1900, China had little ability to undertake serious tasks even within Asia—or even within China—until its own internal problems were resolved. Roosevelt's insistence upon the fiction that China be accorded big power status reduced the credibility of American postwar planning not only in Moscow but also in London.

Roosevelt once reassured his colleagues at the Yalta Conference in February 1945, "that the peace should be written by the Three Powers represented at this table." [14] But none of the really serious questions before the Big Three were settled at Yalta. The "China Tangle" as one historian has called it, had both specific and general significance during and after the war: (1) In specific terms both Britain and Russia suspected that their ally would use China's

---

[12] William C. Bullitt, "How We Won the War and Lost the Peace," *Life*, *XXV* (August 30, 1948): 82–97.
[13] Sherwood, *Roosevelt and Hopkins*, pp. 572–73.
[14] Department of State, *FR: Yalta, 1945*, pp. 589–90.

"faggot" vote on the Big Four in disputes with the former over Asian and colonial questions and with the latter over the postwar organization of Europe. (2) More generally, the notion of China as a member of the Big Power consortium was so obviously out of touch with reality that Churchill and Stalin might well fear that its only purpose was to provide a convenient springboard from the difficult and complicated questions yet to come before the Big Three into the vast uncertainties of "collective security" just as soon as Roosevelt found a way to make sure American interests were fully protected. It had been so in Wilson's vision, and the traditions against serious political involvement still ran strongly in the United States. And in that situation, America's moral and economic power would have their greatest impact. As we shall see later, that is precisely what took place.

Roosevelt also projected vague plans for dismembering and disarming Germany and for extending economic aid to the Soviet Union to assist in its transition back to a peacetime economy. By far the most dramatic response he made to Moscow's opening moves was to promise the formation of a "Second Front" before the end of 1942. It was on this shaky base that all the rest of his diplomacy was constructed. In hopes of forestalling an Anglo-Russian accord that would be unpopular (to say the least) in the United States as well as disruptive of the vital international economic and moral order Henry Luce demanded, the President seized upon apparent assurances George C. Marshall and Harry Hopkins gave him that the British would support a landing in force on the European continent. From later "Cold War" perspectives a few American planners regretted that the President had not struck a bargain with his Allies in 1942, when America's uncommitted potential was a stronger base than the risks of "Second Front" diplomacy. That criticism showed admirable hindsight; it did not help Roosevelt at the time.

Unwilling to do more than support a North African invasion, the Prime Minister confronted the President with a second dilemma interlaced into the first. Roosevelt reluctantly accepted the plan, in part because he felt domestic pressures to justify his

Germany-first strategy. The North African campaign was politically disastrous from beginning to end. It held up production of needed landing craft for a possible 1943 cross-channel operation; it slowed up the delivery of war materials to the Soviet Union; it involved Washington in questionable dealings with the pro-German Vichy French rulers of North Africa; and it kept the United States fighting in a traditionally British sphere of influence (which the British were very anxious to restore) for almost two years.[15] Stalin even charged that the North African campaign had allowed Hitler to move twenty-seven additional divisions to the Eastern Front. Even the small pro-Western group in the Soviet Union, led by Maxim Litvinov and Ivan Maisky, concluded that the United States and Great Britain were planning a strategy which would allow them to restore their own losses on the periphery of Axis power and then dash across Europe after Russia had taken the heart and iron out of the German army.

Against these all but calamitous developments, Roosevelt raised the banner of Axis "Unconditional Surrender" at the Casablanca Conference, much to Churchill's surprise and dismay. It is now clear that the President was addressing Moscow as much as he was Berlin; in fact more so, for he was trying to convince the Soviets that there would be no separate peace in the West and no race for Berlin after the Red Army had beaten the Germans in the East.

The ensuing "Italian Campaign" added yet another twist to the President's political difficulties. The United States could not oblige the Russian demand for a voice in the Allied Control Commission for that country without risking, so they believed, a substantial increase in Russian influence in a nation where the Communist party and its partisan military units already seemed to threaten postwar stability. In the following months American diplomats winced every time the Russians cited the Italian example as precedent and justification for their own unilateral acts in Eastern European countries.

[15] See John Baggueley, "The World War and the Cold War," in David Horowitz (ed.), *Containment and Revolution* (Boston: Beacon Press, 1967), pp. 92–93.

Perceiving the growing impasse quite clearly, Churchill sought to settle with Stalin in the summer of 1944—outside the framework of the Atlantic Charter and other American pronouncements on the peace to come. Roosevelt reluctantly agreed to the Prime Minister's trip to Moscow, but he warned that he could not bind the United States to any decisions that might be reached. "It is important that I retain complete freedom of action after this conference is over," he advised the American Ambassador in the Russian capital.[16]

Roosevelt's caveat notwithstanding, the two European leaders divided up the Balkans according to a complicated formula which really meant that Russia would control Rumania, Hungary, and Bulgaria; they would share control of Yugoslavia; and the British would call the tune in Greece. As Churchill publicly recognized, the Russians stuck to their bargain in Greece, where leftist partisan forces perhaps had the greatest chance to convert the war against Germany into a revolutionary victory over the exiled King and his supporters. Stalin even lent the moral force of his military mission in that country to British purposes. As Anthony Eden recalled, "Colonel Popov's uniform" sitting on the British side of the table had its effect upon the partisan leaders during crucial conferences.[17]

Roosevelt's close advisors were anxious lest these supposedly "temporary" arrangements congealed into hard spheres of influence before the United States could reach these areas with its postwar economic solvents. The State Department prepared an emergency formula for Roosevelt's use at the upcoming Yalta Big Three Conference. They filled their proposed "Declaration on Liberated Europe" with pointed references to the Atlantic Charter, and proposed all the proper machinery to see that these principles were carried into effect within as short a time as possible.

The President had serious doubts about this strategy, particularly concerning the operative commission it posited. He may

---

[16] Sherwood, *Roosevelt and Hopkins*, p. 834.
[17] Anthony Eden, *The Reckoning* (Boston: Houghton Mifflin, 1965), p. 581.

even have been worried that it might militate against the authority of the United Nations.[18] The Russians, as expected, also objected to that part of the "Declaration." After the wording was
changed, eliminating the enforcement mechanism, the proposal
was accepted by the Big Three.[19]

There is a bit more to the story of the Declaration on Liberated Europe at the Yalta Conference. Churchill's angry outburst
when the American Secretary of State read out the proposed
United Nations trusteeship plan—"Under no circumstances would
he ever consent to forty or fifty nations thrusting interfering
fingers into the life's existence of the British Empire"—and his
later warning that he wanted it understood that neither would
he tolerate the misuse of the Declaration on Liberated Europe
in Empire questions, surely inhibited Roosevelt's freedom of action as much as any Russian caveats.

The Prime Minister was merely restating his original objec-
tions to the Atlantic Charter, but at a most inopportune time
from an American point of view. Perhaps Stalin was amused at
this development, or perhaps uninterested, but in any event it
worked to his advantage. On the way home from Yalta, news-
men pressed Roosevelt on the colonial problem, always sure
to bring a response from their readers. The President was sur-
prisingly subdued and cautious. He seemed much less sure that
much could be done immediately about such places as French
Indo-China, though he assured them that he continued to believe
that the colonial era was just about all over. "The Atlantic Charter is a beautiful idea," he remarked cryptically—and left them
to ponder his meaning.

Did this mean that he had finally decided to resolve his central
dilemma by recognizing also the Russian demands in Eastern
Europe? Perhaps so; there are those who make this argument
quite effectively. But if he did mean to do that, he left his successors a cruel task—how to explain his report to Congress on

---

[18] See *FR, Yalta, 1945*, pp. 862 and 919, and especially p. 503 for FDR's ambiguity. Also James F. Byrnes, *Speaking Frankly* (New York: Harper,
1947), p. 33.
[19] *Ibid.*

Yalta. In that speech he said that the Conference spelled the end "of the system of unilateral action and exclusive alliances and spheres of influence and balances of power and all the other expedients which have been tried for centuries—and have failed."

## President Truman Cuts the Tangled Web

About the time of the Yalta Conference several of President Roosevelt's advisors were also turning over the possibilities of using economic leverage directly on the Russians. Roosevelt had early seen the possibilities of using economic aid, in combination with a tough policy on Germany, to draw the Soviet Union into postwar plans. But though he had initiated talks with the Russians, he had not become deeply involved in them, or interfered when they stalled in bureaucratic corridors outside the White House. Treasury Secretary Morgenthau proposed a plan for extending a ten billion dollar credit to the Soviet Union on the grounds that the British had already been assured that there would be American aid for them after the war, and that such an offer would do much to clear up suspicions among the Big Three.

This matter was before the President when word came from Moscow that Molotov had asked Ambassador Harriman about a possible six billion dollar credit. Harriman did not much like the way the request had been put. "Having in mind the repeated statements of American public figures concerning the desirability of receiving extensive large Soviet orders for the postwar and transition period," read the Russian note, "the Soviet Government considers it possible to place orders on the basis of long term credits to the amount of six billion dollars." Though it was true that several "public figures" had indeed made such statements about the Russian market (including the ambassador himself), Harriman objected to the way it sounded coming from Molotov. Nevertheless, he was convinced that the Russians really wanted the credits. His own position was that the United States should use the request in such a way so that "at the appropriate time the Russians should be given to understand that our willingness to cooperate wholeheartedly with them in their vast reconstruction problems will depend upon their behavior in international matters."

The State Department agreed that the ambassador had taken the proper "tactical point of view" of the matter—in opposition to Morgenthau's soft approach—and that dollar diplomacy might be the answer to all those who felt that American liberalism was acquiescing in an Anglo-Russian reorganization of the prewar, patchwork colonial and spheres-of-influence system, which had failed so miserably in the interwar years.

Roosevelt decided that the issue "should not be pressed further" until he had an opportunity to speak directly with Stalin and other Soviet officials at Yalta. No such discussions took place at the Big Three meeting, even though the Russians hinted once or twice in the course of the talks that they would like to take up the subject. On the other hand, Roosevelt committed himself to very large reparations for the Soviets from postwar Germany, much to the dismay of Prime Minister Churchill.

Ambassador Harriman may have interpreted Roosevelt's maneuvering at Yalta on these questions as a signal that he had come over fully to his point of view, especially since the reparations matter was so full of uncertainties. In any event, when he was called home to brief President Truman on Russian–American relations immediately after Roosevelt's death, he referred to this subject at once. Recalling his original irritation at the way in which the request had been worded, he added that "there were some quarters in Moscow that believed it was a matter of life and death to American business to increase our exports to Russia." Putting it as strongly as possible, the ambassador told Truman that we were faced with a "barbarian invasion of Europe." The President assured Harriman, not once but several times, in the course of their conversation that he intended to be "firm" with the Russians.[20]

The main political issue at the moment was the composition of the provisional government of Poland. Each side was claiming

---

[20] *FR, Yalta, 1945,* pp. 309–23; Harry S. Truman, *Memoirs* (New York: Doubleday, 1965 ed.), pp. 86, 95–99.

that the other had abandoned the Yalta agreements. But the Russians, now in possession of the country, had acted to legitimize its creation, the Lublin Government, by signing a formal security treaty with it which they insisted had the same status as one recently concluded with France.

After hearing the different views of his closest advisors, Truman decided to be "firm" with Foreign Minister Molotov, who was scheduled to see him before going on to the United Nations Conference in San Francisco. When Molotov entered the President's office, Truman hardly let him get settled before relieving himself emotionally of all the advice he had been getting since Roosevelt's death. Declaring that the Russians had willfully violated the Yalta agreement on Poland as well as the Declaration on Liberated Europe, the President of twelve days handed Molotov a message for Stalin which warned that the United States had gone as far as it could to meet Soviet wishes already, and would not be a party to any further consultations if Russia did not promise the establishment of a "new Provisional Government of National Unity genuinely representative of the democratic elements of the Polish people."

Like many of the wartime Big Three pronouncements, the Yalta protocol on Poland was subject to two interpretations. When this fact had been brought to Roosevelt's attention by Admiral William D. Leahy, the former President had replied, "I know Bill—I know it. But it's the best I can do for Poland at this time." Truman (with Leahy's urging) had evidently decided that the time had come to do more for Poland—and the rest of Eastern Europe.[21] In the protocol there were all the proper references to a "strong, free, independent, and democratic Poland," but these were more than balanced by the operative clause which said only that the Lublin government should be "reorganized on a broader democratic basis." Hence Leahy's original dismay and his comment to Roosevelt that it was "so elastic that the Russians

---

[21] William D. Leahy, *I Was There* (New York: Whittlesey House, 1950), pp. 315–16.

can stretch it all the way from Yalta to Washington without ever technically breaking it."

Truman always insisted that he was carrying out Roosevelt's plan for the postwar world. The trouble was that it was not only as elastic as the Yalta agreement on Poland, but as unfinished as, say, the Chinese Revolution in 1945. "President Roosevelt," Truman wrote "had built up the idea that China was a great power because he looked to the future and wanted to encourage the Chinese people. In reality it would be only with the greatest difficulty that Chiang Kai-shek could even reoccupy South China." [22] Truman's sober description of the specific illusions and realities he encountered in the Far Eastern situation should also recall the more general problems posed by Roosevelt's insistence upon including China in the Big Power group, and the suspicions this part of his "plan" engendered in British and Russian minds.

In the course of the April 23 lecture to the Russian Foreign Minister, the President had referred obliquely to the question of economic aid from the United States after the war, implying that there would be none unless the Russians changed their ways promptly. This admonition was given more substance a few weeks later when Washington abruptly cut off Lend-Lease aid following the German surrender. From one point of view it can be argued that Russia had little right to complain; after all, the United States had already given Moscow more than eleven billion dollars in such aid. The argument really begs the question since (1) the Soviets had more than paid their way in absorbing the greatest blows of Nazi Germany in blood and treasure, and (2) both sides knew that there would be a new account sheet started after the war, based on trial political balances.

Truman wanted to sensitize the Russians to America's economic ability to reward its friends and discourage its adversaries. Stalin's equally blunt reactions indicated the "test" had succeeded. At Potsdam the political issue shifted to Polish boundary questions.

---

[22] Truman, *Memoirs, II*, pp. 61–62.

Moscow had assigned the provisional government a favorable western border well into what had been Eastern Germany, without consulting its allies. Truman shifted his emphasis to reparations:

> The President stated that he had no objection to an expression of opinion regarding the western frontiers, however, he wanted it distinctly understood that the zones of occupation will be as established. Any other course will make reparations very difficult, particularly if part of the German territory is gone before agreement is reached on what reparations should be.

> Stalin replied that the Soviet Union was not afraid of the reparations question and would if necessary renounce them.[23]

The Kremlin had no intention of giving up reparations from Germany, of course. What the Soviet dictator was replying to was the President's April 23 message conveyed to him through Molotov. One translation of that reply would be: "Do your worst, the Polish government and boundary questions are not debatable any longer!"

Apparently on his own, and certainly with much less advice from Ambassador Harriman and the others, the President had devised a second "test" of Russian intentions which he brought with him to the Potsdam Conference that July. At one of the early plenary sessions Stalin put forward a demand for revision of the international convention governing access to and control of the Turkish Straits. During the era of the *Pax Brittanica*, the Foreign Office kept a close watch over the Dardanelles to make sure the Russians did not slip through that waterway and spread throughout the Mediterranean. It was still Foreign Office policy, whether Anthony Eden or Ernest Bevin was in charge.

Both Britain and Russia were anxious, therefore, to hear from the United States on this controversy. By itself, Great Britain was in no position to sustain the surveillance for very long, while the Soviet Union very much wanted American blessing for a revision of the convention. Truman was ready: he read his two colleagues a paper previously prepared on the question of major

---

[23] State Department, *FR, Potsdam Papers, II*, p. 209.

European waterways that bordered on two or more states, such as the Rhine and the Danube, and he suggested that it might also apply to the Dardanelles. His proposal called for free and unrestricted navigation "of such inland waterways as border on two or more states," under the supervision of the Big Five and the riparian states concerned.

In his *Memoirs* Truman said that he had long been thinking about how political problems in Europe going back hundreds of years might now be solved "by linking up the breadbasket with the industrial centers through a free flow of trade." "To facilitate this flow," he continued, "the Rhine and the Danube could be linked with a vast network of canals which would provide a passage all the way from the North Sea to the Black Sea and the Mediterranean." [24]

Truman also wrote that he had intended to extend this proposal to the Suez and Panama Canals, but it is important to keep in mind that his original proposal made no mention of this plan. In fact the wording excluded those key British and American sea passages by definition. According to the minutes of the Potsdam Conference he mentioned only the Danube and the Turkish Straits, both previously of strategic concern to the Soviet Union. Speaking for the British Empire, Churchill specifically excluded the Suez Canal—without contradiction from Truman even after Molotov pressed him on this matter. Suez and Panama were also protected by military bases: Truman added that his plan for the Danube and the Turkish Straits "did not contemplate any fortifications of any kind." [25]

It is difficult to see how any Russian leader, Czar or Communist dictator, whatever his ideological foundations or personal psychological quirks, could have responded to this proposal favorably. Even if Truman had brought Alexander Kerensky from the Hoover Library to sit in Stalin's place, the answer would no doubt have been the same. With China's vote every key question in such a commission might go against Russia's interests. How

---

[24] Truman, *Memoirs,* pp. 263, 415.
[25] *FR, Potsdam Papers, II,* pp. 654, 303–304, 366.

could that be tolerated in a bipolar world by either side, especially when basic political questions concerning the nations bordering on the Danube had yet to be explored, let alone resolved?

But Truman interpreted the "test" results as conclusive: "I had proposed the internationalization of all the principal waterways. Stalin did not want this. What Stalin wanted was control of the Black Sea Straits and the Danube. The Russians were planning world conquest." [26]

## Public Diplomacy with an Atomic Flavor

The Big Three had agreed at Potsdam that discussions of peace treaties with former enemy states should begin at the first postwar meeting of the Foreign Ministers' Council which assembled in London in mid-September. Secretary of War Henry L. Stimson was anxious lest these talks begin under the charged atmosphere created by the atomic bombs dropped on Hiroshima and Nagasaki to end the Pacific war. When he talked about his concern with Secretary of State James F. Byrnes, he found him preoccupied and "very much against any attempt to cooperate with Russia." The secretary's mind, Stimson confided privately to his diary, was full "of his problems with the coming meeting of the foreign ministers and he looks to having the presence of the bomb in his pocket, so to speak, as a great weapon to get through the thing he has." [27]

Stimson himself had only recently come to the position he was advocating—a direct approach to the Soviets on development and control of atomic energy combined with an offer to share information—to both Byrnes and President Truman. He felt it should be attempted before trying to deal with political questions because, as he said in a memorandum to Truman, the atomic bomb had come to dominate all political questions. At Potsdam, however, Stimson had still been urging the President to make use of this "master card" to reassert the Open Door policy in Eastern

---

[26] Truman, *Memoirs*, p. 455.
[27] Diary entry, September 4, 1945: *The Papers of Henry L. Stimson*, Yale University, New Haven, Connecticut.

Europe and Manchuria. "Atomic diplomacy" did not begin at the moment when news first reached Truman at Potsdam of the successful atomic test in New Mexico; nor did it originate some weeks earlier when Stimson told the new President that the atomic bomb would have consequences (Byrnes added dominance) "on our present foreign relations." That Truman delayed the Potsdam meeting in order to have this trump card in his hand when he met Stalin has been asserted with strong supporting evidence in recent years. [28] Long before any serious revisionist studies had been published, Truman's personal secretary noted almost casually in a book of highly subjective recollections that the President had told him just before meeting the Soviet delegation, "If it explodes, as I think it will, I'll certainly have a hammer on those boys!" [29]

Unfortunately, overemphasis upon such rediscovered evidence can, and I believe has, reduced our perspective on the origins of the Cold War to the dimensions of Truman's personality. Far more revealing about how the bomb influenced American foreign policy attitudes in general was Truman's reaction on board the *Augusta* after Potsdam to the bombing of Hiroshima: "This is the greatest thing in history. It's time for us to get home." [30] By no means did this imply only a simple negative diplomacy aimed at the Soviet Union. The United States relied on the bomb as the security backing for the new United Nations; and Washington was critical of all those who did not see this so clearly, whether they were viewing things from Moscow or Paris or even from London.

Stimson's new position on the control of atomic energy had actually evolved from a question about the proposed United Nations. Back in January the Secretary of War had first become concerned that the United States was about to repeat a mistake it had made at the end of World War I. Washington had tried once before to build a world organization based almost solely

---

[28] See Gar Alperovitz, *Atomic Diplomacy: Hiroshima and Potsdam* (New York: Simon & Schuster, 1965).
[29] *Ibid.*, p. 130.
[30] Truman, *Memoirs*, p. 465.

upon its own moral leadership, before establishing tangible political and economic guarantees. When President Wilson finally recognized this, Stimson noted, he "proposed a joint covenant of guarantee by Britain and America of the security of France as the pillar of western Europe."

> But the mistake was made of not securing that guarantee before the second step of creating the League of Nations whose safety was in large part to be dependent upon such a guarantee. As a result the League of Nations lacked a foundation of security which ultimately proved fatal to it.[31]

Stimson had then recommended to the Secretary of State that the United States offer a "covenant of guarantee" to the Soviet Union against a German resurgence. This proposal was actually taken up by Byrnes when the London Foreign Ministers' Conference failed nine months later—after the world had entered the atomic era.

In January and February of 1945, Byrnes, then an aide to President Roosevelt, was far more worried about the old Wilsonian dream of open diplomacy and open covenants of peace. Though faithful to the late President to the end, Byrnes could not conceal his troubled state of mind and obvious distaste for Big Three diplomacy. At Yalta, he told several congressional leaders, Stalin had kept repeating, "If the three of us stick together, we can maintain the peace of the world." The only unity he foresaw in such diplomacy would come when the United States finally yielded to Soviet demands.[32]

Both Stimson and Byrnes, on the other hand, frequently discussed the atomic bomb's likely influence on postwar international problems, and particularly how it might be used to make the Russians more manageable in Europe. Both men sat on the Interim Committee appointed by Truman to decide what to do with the first bombs that came out of the scientific-industrial assembly

---

[31] *FR, 1945, I*, pp. 23–27.
[32] Burton K. Wheeler to Oswald Garrison Villard, February 21, 1945: *The Papers of Oswald Garrison Villard*, Houghton Library, Harvard University, Cambridge, Massachusetts.

line. "We were under incredible pressure to get it done before the Potsdam meeting," said J. Robert Oppenheimer several years later. And on June 1, 1945, the Interim Committee's "discussion resolved around the question raised by Secretary Stimson as to whether there was any hope at all of using this development to get less barbarous relations with the Russians." [33]

After Potsdam these two policymakers divided sharply on how to achieve their common purpose. Another atomic scientist was appalled by Byrnes's "sense of proportion" and was upset that Truman had decided to name him Secretary of State. "I shared Byrnes's concern about Russia's throwing around her weight in the postwar period," wrote Leo Szilard, "but I was completely flabbergasted by the assumption that rattling the bomb might make Russian more manageable."

> I began to doubt that there was any way for me to communicate with Byrnes in this matter, and my doubt became certainty when he turned to me and said, "Well, you come from Hungary—you would not want Russia to stay in Hungary indefinitely." I certainly didn't want Russia to stay in Hungary indefinitely, but what Byrnes said offended my sense of proportion. I was concerned at this point that by demonstrating the bomb and using it in the war against Japan, we might start an atomic arms race between America and Russia which might end with the destruction of both countries. I was *not* disposed at this point to worry about what would happen to Hungary.[34]

Secretary Byrnes gave Hungary and Rumania high priority at the London meeting. He was not only disposed to worry about what happened to them specifically, but he also believed that what happened in Bucharest and Budapest would largely determine the shape of postwar diplomacy and either strengthen or weaken the United Nations. Soon after the discussions began at London, when it became evident that Byrnes had no intention

---

[33] Atomic Energy Commission, *In the Matter of J. Robert Oppenheimer* (Washington: Government Printing Office, 1954), pp. 31–38.
[34] Szilard, *Reminiscences* in Donald Fleming and Bernard Bailyn (eds.), *Perspectives in American History*, II (Cambridge: Harvard University Press, 1968), pp. 94–151.

of changing Truman's Potsdam position on recognition of the new governments in Soviet-controlled Eastern Europe, Foreign Minister Molotov challenged the right of China and France to participate in the debates over the peace treaties for those countries.

The Secretary of State quickly turned this maneuver to his own advantage, emphasizing that the question of spheres of influence and collective security was at stake. At this moment Byrnes used the "springboard" Roosevelt had provided in public rhetoric about the Big Four, now the Big Five (with the addition of France), and leaped into the deep waters of collective security, buoyed up by America's monopoly over atomic energy. Pointing out that Russia had twice agreed, first at Potsdam, then again a few days before at the outset of the conference, that France and China should take part, he generalized the American position into a defense of the rights of all small nations to share in the peace-making. All that the Russian Foreign Minister could say in reply was that the original decision had been a "mistake."

By now the Russian–American disagreement was in the papers and public diplomacy (which meant no diplomacy) became the rule. The Secretary of State suggested a "compromise" proposal by which France and China would be excluded in preliminary treaty discussions. But, in a second stage of deliberations the treaties would have to be submitted to a general peace conference composed of the members of the United Nations Security Council, all European members of that organization, and all non-European members who had supplied substantial military contingents against Germany and Italy.

Discussions stalled at that point, but the Secretary of State felt he had good reason to be pleased. "Our stand at London required them to make a reevaluation," he asserted. It was a true test of wills: America's desire to build collective security in one world against the Soviet insistence upon spheres of influence. "Our attitude was a shock to them. . . . Our fight to have France and China remain in the council was generally applauded, and our fight for the peace conference and for the right of the smaller states to participate in the peace won for us the good opinion of those states. And it forced the Soviets to begin to reorient their policy." [35]

Byrnes seemed confident that this reorientation process would ultimately further American interests, and his optimism appeared to be well-founded when the Soviets did finally agree to a general peace conference to be held in Paris. On the other hand, President Truman thought Byrnes made too many concessions at a special Big Three Foreign Ministers' meeting in Moscow in December 1945, in order to get Stalin's grudging assent to any conference at all. The Secretary yielded the point of diplomatic recognition in some instances—as far as he was concerned it had served its purpose already—and the Russians refused to accept any more than twenty-one nations for the Paris Conference. The real issue, left unsettled, was whether these twenty-one would simply ratify prior decisions of the Big Three, or attempt to exercise independent judgment. And that would depend in turn upon what lead the United States provided since it was the most interested in public diplomacy.

On August 6, 1946, Secretary Byrnes addressed the Conference and delivered an indictment of spheres of influence, ticking off the steps taken by the Soviet Union to maintain Big Three dominance. Then the United States joined with a majority of the other nations in voting ninety-four recommendations back to the Council of Foreign Ministers. Accompanying the Secretary of State to the Paris meeting were two of his former colleagues from the Senate, Tom Connally and Arthur H. Vandenberg. Each enjoyed a good deal of influence in that body. Connally was sometimes called "the Godfather of the United Nations;" Vandenberg was in a special category of recent converts to Republican "internationalism." In fact he was its most dramatic representative and highly prized by the administration.

Connally was uneasy at Paris. The shouting match between the United States and the Soviet Union threatened the very existence of the United Nations. "Its original job was not to *make* peace," he remarked in a radio interview, "but to preserve and

---

[35] Byrnes, *Speaking Frankly*, pp. 102–105.

extend peace after it has been reestablished." The Texas Senator had put his finger on the change in strategy away from Big Three diplomacy wrought by Byrnes at London the previous fall, but he offered no real solution to the problem. Perhaps there was none. As he noted, his distinction posited "a rather artificial division of labor." [36]

Committed to total public diplomacy, the piling up of useless majorities against the Soviet Union in widely publicized conferences and in the UN, while waiting for the Russian Empire to crumble in Eastern Europe, Byrnes was unconcerned with Connally's inner musings one way or the other. Senator Arthur Vandenberg was also free of any troubled feelings about America's course at the meetings. His credo was rigid adherence to the Atlantic Charter and the Declaration on Liberated Europe—at least so far as these pronouncements applied to Russia's policies in Eastern Europe and the British Empire. Any compromise was appeasement. "No more Munichs!" the Senator wrote in April 1946. "If it is to be impossible for us to get along with the Soviets on such a basis, the quicker we find it out the better. America must behave like the Number One World Power which she is. Ours must be the world's moral leadership—or the world won't have any." [37]

At Paris Vandenberg returned to the subject of free navigation on the Danube, leading a successful fight for a "majority" resolution in support of Truman's Potsdam plan. He also took up the cause of equal opportunity and nondiscrimination in the draft treaty for Rumania. Directing his attack towards recent Soviet bilateral treaties with several Eastern European countries, the Senator reiterated words and phrases which had come down from earlier American diplomatic exchanges over the Open Door policy. "We call on the Conference," the Senator concluded with a flourish, "to endorse the economic provisions of the Atlantic Charter, to which we have all subscribed. . . ." [38]

---

[36] Department of State, *Bulletin, XV* (August 4, 1946), 206–207.
[37] Arthur H. Vandenberg, Jr. (ed.), *The Private Papers of Senator Vandenberg* (Boston: Houghton Mifflin, 1952), p. 267.
[38] Department of State, *Bulletin, XV* (October 20, 1946), 712–13.

At least two nations taking a leading part at Paris—Great Britain and the Soviet Union—had never really subscribed to the economic or political provisions of the Atlantic Charter. Their qualified acceptances were enough for the senator and for Byrnes, however. Molotov attempted two responses to this attack, neither of which swayed any votes to the Russian side. First, he charged that the United States was replacing Great Britain as the leading "imperialist" power of the world, extending its military tentacles everywhere it could and encouraging opposition to Russia in the Balkans and the Mediterranean area. Second, he asserted that the "open door" policy was a facade, masking American intentions to exploit the small nations of the world:

> It is surely not so difficult to understand that if American capital were given a free hand in the small states ruined and enfeebled by the war, as the advocates of the principle of "equal opportunity" desire, American capital would buy up the local industries, appropriate the more attractive Rumanian, Yugoslav and all other enterprises, and would become the master in these small states.[39]

The Foreign Minister's solicitous concern for the economic independence of Rumania and Yugoslavia stemmed from two main sources. The first was the situation the Russians found in Eastern Europe as their troops drove the Germans out of Rumania and Hungary. In these countries the Germans had shaped the economies to serve the Nazi war machine; when they left, there was often no one to take over, the previous owners and managers having already been removed or killed. The initial problem for Russian policymakers was to prevent these economies from being controlled by a potential enemy. A second source of concern was the Kremlin's still unfinished plans for reorienting Eastern European economic and political currents in more favorable directions for Russian postwar recovery. In part these plans depended upon other outside aid and reparations.

Molotov's crude rendition of Marxism-Leninism changed nobody's mind at Paris. Few American leaders seriously believed

---

[39] V. M. Molotov, *Problems of Foreign Policy* (Moscow: Foreign Languages Publishing House, 1949), pp. 214 *ff*.

that East European markets and investments were worth all that fuss for any immediate benefit they might have to American postwar economic problems. The Russians, on the other hand, were fearful that even one major foreign investor—as in the case of the British-American oil companies in prewar Rumania—would exercise an undue influence in government circles and deprive the Russians of access to this key resource. For their part, Americans did believe that the resumption of normal prewar, East-West trade (and its improvement as Truman envisioned in his Potsdam paper) was essential to the full recovery of Europe, and thus important generally to American wellbeing and security.

In addition to these difficulties, the Paris Conference was interrupted several times by outside issues which had a deleterious influence on its deliberations: Secretary Byrnes's famous "Stuttgart Speech" seemed to reopen the Polish-German frontier question; Secretary of Commerce Henry Wallace's Madison Square Garden attack on Byrnes's policies created a moment of confusion, and set trans-Atlantic cables humming with the latter's protests to Washington. And in New York the United Nations Atomic Energy Commission was getting nowhere in the debate over the American "Baruch Plan."

Senator Vandenberg followed the New York debate closely while the Paris meetings reached a climax over America's insistence on the Open Door policy in Eastern Europe. Vandenberg immediately connected the two issues. "It is *the* 'showdown' with Moscow." [40]

Stimson's argument for a direct, bilateral, approach to the Soviet Union on atomic energy had been rejected in favor of a presentation through the United Nations. President Truman had then requested Bernard M. Baruch to submit the American plan; Baruch promptly amended all previous schemes by insisting that the veto power would have to be suspended in all phases of international atomic questions, and particularly from any votes on how to punish atomic lawbreakers. Once again the United States

---

[40] Arthur H. Vandenberg, Jr. (ed.), *The Private Papers of Senator Vandenberg* (Boston: Houghton Mifflin, 1952), p. 291.

sought a "majority vote" diplomacy; and once again the Soviets charged this was a break with Big Three understandings. "Is it not in order to free the hands of admirers of the atomic bomb," asserted Molotov, "that certain people are raising such a to-do about the 'veto'?" [41]

Baruch had long been convinced that the United Nations would have to prove its effectiveness as a peace-making and peace-keeping organization *before* there could be any elimination or surrender of American atomic weapons to international control. The "Baruch Plan" therefore was an attempt to make the United Nations effective through atomic diplomacy, though had the Soviets accepted it, the atomic arms race might have been avoided. One may regret that they did not and still insist Stimson's was the more realistic alternative in the situation. The Russians also charged that the 1946 atomic tests at Bikini atoll in the Pacific demonstrated that no negotiations could take place so long as only one party had the bomb. Baruch admitted to Truman that his stand would cut into "the general . . . veto power. . . . I told him that some people thought it might be bad if we put that [elimination of the veto power] in because that would stop the negotiations. . . . But of what use," Baruch continued, "is a treaty, if there is no way of enforcing it?" "I quite agree with you," replied Truman emphatically. The President then made "a statement regarding the veto power, which showed that he thought it was a mistake. He said that if Harry Stimson had been backed up in Manchuria there would have been no war." [42] This typical reference to the failure of collective security in the 1930's with its resultant creation of large, aggressively nationalistic, political-economic blocs helps to explain the historical lenses through which American leaders viewed the world in 1945, and much of the time since then.

[41] Molotov, *Problems of Foreign Policy* (Moscow: Foreign Languages Publishing House, 1949), pp. 251–52.
[42] Baruch to James F. Byrnes, March 13, 1946 and "BMB Memorandum of Meeting on June 7, 1946 with the President and J. F. Byrnes," *The Papers of Bernard M. Baruch*, Firestone Library, Princeton University, Princeton, New Jersey.

In the United Nations commission, the Russian delegate complained that Baruch was presenting a plan with no recourse, and that he was doing this at a time when there was "no agreement, no convention, no guarantee forbidding the production and use of atomic weapons. I don't see how we can ask states blindly to believe in the good intentions of the United States and to accept, without query, the United States proposal as regards atom weapons." [43] The Russian counterproposal for an immediate convention against the use of atomic bombs and the destruction of existing weapons merely demonstrated the total unreality of trying to settle outstanding issues in a commission where the Soviet Union and Canada and Poland had an equal vote. The real issue was not even the Baruch Plan, but the ultimate usefulness of United Nations diplomacy.

Though peace treaties were finally negotiated and ratified with the former German satellites, the process had not strengthened the United Nations. As Senator Connally pointed out, the United Nations had been conceived of as a peace-keeping organization, not a peace-making body. There was no way of converting it into the latter without abandoning the former, and risking "Cold War" or perhaps worse. In part this was the result of basic ambiguities in postwar planning: The big power veto was incompatible with any other interpretation, but the presence of France and China in the big power consortium added uncertainties which were difficult to assess then as now. The veto power presumed there was a consensus among the Big Three or the Big Five on the terms of the peace when there really were underlying disagreements. Without doubt America's postwar planning was the most far-reaching. It requires no "revisionist" argument or insight to see that American policymakers were the most interested, as they had been in Paris, to extend the area of their international order, and that they believed that political regionalism and spheres of influence led to the creation of a sterling bloc, a rouble bloc, and a dollar bloc. [44]

---

[43] Quoted by John M. Hancock in a letter to Dean Acheson, August 15, 1946.
[44] Byrnes, *Speaking Frankly*, p. 155.

## Ideologies and Political Economies

Louis Halle, a former State Department planner, has expanded our awareness of the historical vision shared by American policy-makers at the outset of the "Cold War" era.

> From the beginning of the 1930's to almost the end of 1962, the populations of the West lived continuously in a terrible fear. The general economic breakdown of 1929–1930, which foreboded the breakdown of the social order everywhere, was followed by the rise of Hitler and the Japanese warlords, to the point where it no longer seemed possible to stop them. The terrors of World War II were followed by those associated with the prospect of an imminent general breakdown of civilization and the oblitera- tion of all that made life worth living, or even possible, under the Muscovite tyranny that was spreading from the East.

Halle suggests that one read J.R.R. Tolkien's now famous trilogy, *The Lord of the Rings,* "which enshrines the mood and the emotion of those long years in which we, in the West, saw almost no possibility of saving ourselves from the intolerable darkness that was overspreading the world from the East." [45]

Communism's appeal as an alternative system vying for world leadership was America's nightmare. And in this dark dream, Russian military forces marched forth into the confusion left by internal subversion. As the Cold War intensified, there grad- ually emerged that near-medieval gothic vision described by Halle. But even in 1945 usually less susceptible men shuddered before the sight. "The greatest crime of Hitler," Ambassador Harriman told James Forrestal in July, "was that his actions had resulted in opening the gates of Eastern Europe to Asia. . . ." [46]

Descriptions of Russian fears are not so readily available; but Stalin's 1947 interview with Harold Stassen might be read in this way:

> Things are not bad in the United States. America is protected by two oceans. In the north there is a weak country, and to the

---

[45] Louis Halle, *The Cold War as History* (London: Chatto & Windus, 1967), p. 138.
[46] Millis (ed.), *The Forrestal Diaries* (New York: Viking Press, 1951), p. 79.

south a weak country, Mexico, and so you need not be afraid of them. After the War of Independence, the United States did not have another war for sixty years and that was a great help to the rapid development of the United States of America. America's population is made up of such people as fled from monarchy, and tyranny and kings and landed aristocracy, and that was also a great help, and that is why America developed in leaps and bounds.[47]

With Russia's two traditional enemies, Germany and Japan, in ashes, perhaps there was no foundation for Stalin's fears except his own paranoid preoccupations. "A freely elected government in any of these [East European] countries," he once exclaimed, "would be anti-Soviet, and that we cannot allow." [48] Determined to have his way in Eastern Europe, Stalin resented American and British pressure because of his own "restraint" in the Italian and Greek situations. There were several indications that the Kremlin was reemphasizing the ideological differences between East and West. No doubt some of this was intended to supply a protective coating to the Red Army to save it from ideological impurities as it came in contact with alien ideas in foreign countries. The Russian dictator had himself once told Yugoslav Communists: "This war is not as in the past; whoever occupies a territory also imposes his own system as far as his army can reach. It cannot be otherwise." [49]

Yet if Stalin could invoke "Our Marxists" whenever it suited him, he could also suspend their prophecies almost at will. He stood before a map of Russia and Eastern Europe and warned these same Yugoslav comrades against pushing the British and Americans: "They will never accept the idea that so great a space should be red, never, never!" [50] Stalin himself had engaged

---

[47] Published in Raymond Dennett and Robert K. Turner (eds.), *Documents on American Foreign Relations, IX* (Princeton: Princeton University Press, 1949), p. 616.
[48] Herz, *Beginnings of the Cold War*, p. 140.
[49] Milovan Djilas, *Conversations With Stalin* (New York: Harcourt, Brace & World, 1962), p. 114.
[50] *Ibid.*, p. 74.

in a fateful dispute with the "permanent revolution" advocates among the first generation Bolsheviks, and emerged with the support necessary to begin "socialism in one country" and the five-year plans.

Russia's first aim in Poland and East Germany, it is now clear, was to close off the gate that had been forced twice in the last generation by German armies. By pushing Polish national frontiers to the West, the Russians secured a territorial margin, and created a client state which would have to rely upon Moscow's good will in order to protect its boundaries against a resurgent Germany. This was true whether or not Poland became a full Communist state. Elsewhere in Eastern Europe, the Kremlin followed variations of this policy.

Soviet goals in East Germany in the months following the Nazi surrender did not include the establishment of farm collectives—Stalin once remarked that communism fit Germany like a saddle fit a cow—but to give land to a new peasant class which would "support whatever government protected them against the possibility of a return of the old owners." [51] Inevitably Russian policy and the men who executed it behaved according to modes and manners used at home, just as the American occupation of West Germany returned to well-known and familiar principles. Germany's separation into walled political zones was brought about originally by the division of the occupation responsibilities, but Secretary Byrnes's final proposal that each power should take 85 per cent of its reparations claims out of its own zone certainly added economic depth to the political barriers. Russia's inconsistent economic policy in Germany revealed the difficulties the Soviets were having in making up their minds on all these questions.

"Nations that will not do business with one another or try to exclude one another from doing business with other countries are not likely in the long run to be good neighbors," affirmed

---

[51] J. P. Nettl, *Eastern Zone and Soviet Policy in Germany* (New York: Oxford University Press, 1951), pp. 85–86.

Secretary Byrnes, even after he had helped to seal Germany's division. "An economic bloc means the regimentation of international commerce," Assistant Secretary of State Will Clayton advised the National Farm Institute. "Foreign trade and domestic trade are one and inseparable," Under Secretary of State Dean Acheson explained to the National Association of Manufacturers. "We cannot expect domestic prosperity under our system without a constantly expanding trade with other nations *and between* other nations." [52]

These comments underscored what American leaders sought to do with their "second chance" at world leadership at the end of World War II. The authors of *The Political Economy of American Foreign Policy* wrote:

> The United States used its great wartime and postwar influence in a wholehearted effort to turn back the tides of economic nationalism which had run so strongly in the interwar years. This effort was guided by an explicit set of ideas about the kind of world economic order toward which American policy was working. The intention was to recreate an integrated and—as far as possible—automatic world economy, largely free of interference by national governments, on the model of the 19th-century system, as it was conventionally understood. [53]

Weaker capitalist nations such as France and Great Britain had great difficulties in surviving this American "effort," and were saved only with the advent of the Marshall Plan in 1947. But though Americans had to amend some of their assumptions about the "automatic world economy," their goals remained the same. An immediate reversal of Soviet policy in Eastern Europe had not proved possible, as we have seen, short of military force, an unacceptable risk even in the days of atomic monopoly. The famous Mr. "X" article provided a rationale for "containing" the Muscovite tyranny, and eventually forcing therein a break-

---

[52] Department of State, *Bulletin, XIII* (November 18, 1945): 784 ff., *XIV* (February 24, 1946): 273–76 and *Vital Speeches, XI* (February 1, 1945): 263–65.
[53] William Y. Elliott, *et al., The Political Economy of American Foreign Policy* (New York: Holt, 1955), p. 206.

down or mellowing of its power—without war. The liberation of Eastern Europe was put off for the time being, and fortunately became symbolic instead of substantive. In that sense the "containment policy" was useful in dampening the prospects of a hot war, but its use of military and ideological images had very nearly the opposite effect.

These images dramatized American fears concerning the existence of large Communist parties in Italy and France, and, in some minds, even extended to the election of a Labor government in England committed to severe restrictions on private property and to the nationalization of key industries. The idea that the Soviet Union constituted a serious military threat to the United States in 1945 has now been largely discounted. But as American leaders rushed from their tents to put on their ideological armor against the "Red Peril," military rearmament and atomic saber-rattling was also inevitable.

The 1948 Czechoslovakian *coup d'état,* the Berlin Blockade, the "loss" of China, the Korean War, all in rapid succession buried realities under the trampling rush to unfurl ideological banners on the plain where "civilization" met the charging hordes from hither Asia. Of the two major powers surviving World War II, by any calculation the United States was the strongest. To it belonged the diplomatic and ideological initiative; but John Foster Dulles was not alone seven years later in believing that America was losing the ideological battle. He blamed it on the "containment" policy, and over-close association with Great Britain and France—static powers in a dynamic world. Others supported General Eisenhower in 1952 because they believed that Truman and his Secretary of State and the Democratic Party had become enslaved by their own Cold War rhetoric. But the great majority of Americans voted simply for a man who promised the best chance for a way out of the Korean War. Whatever else divided them, this majority felt that "limited wars" were not the answer to the Soviet challenge.

But the Cold War survived the Korean conflict and Stalin's death, transfigured into a battle for the Third World. Though it distressed some liberal Democratic policymakers of earlier years,

Secretary Dulles even managed to make older "containment" wine suit the new bottles of "liberation" rhetoric. Eventually, however, growing defections among liberals became open rebellion as the prolonged struggle in Vietnam eroded their past assumptions about the nature of the Cold War.

The effort to undo the work of the early mythmakers will involve overstatement, imprecision, and misinterpretation. This is to be expected. But already it has broadened our understanding of the recent past in significant measure.

# 2

# Arthur Schlesinger, Jr.

*The son of a distinguished historian, Arthur Schlesinger, Jr. was born in Columbus, Ohio in 1915. Educated at Harvard, he won a Pulitzer Prize in 1945 for* The Age of Jackson *(Boston: Little, Brown and Co.). Among his more recent publications are three volumes in* The Age of Roosevelt *(Boston: Houghton Mifflin, 1957–1960),* A Thousand Days: John F. Kennedy in the White House *(Boston: Houghton Mifflin, 1965),* The Bitter Heritage: Vietnam and American Democracy *(Boston: Houghton Mifflin, 1967), and* The Crisis of Confidence *(Boston: Houghton Mifflin, 1969). During 1961–1964 Mr. Schlesinger served as a special assistant to Presidents Kennedy and Johnson. He currently holds the Albert Schweitzer Chair in the Humanities at The City University of New York.*

*The present essay appeared originally in* Foreign Affairs, XLVI *(October 1967), pp. 22–52, copyright © 1967 by the Council on Foreign Relations, Inc., New York, and is reprinted here by special permission.*

**T**he Cold War in its original form was a presumably mortal antagonism, arising in the wake of the Second World War, between two rigidly hostile blocs, one led by the Soviet Union, the other by the United States. For nearly two somber and dangerous decades this antagonism dominated the fears of mankind; it may even, on occasion, have come close to blowing up the planet. In recent years, however, the once implacable struggle has lost its familiar clarity of outline. With the passing of old issues and the emergence of new conflicts and contestants, there is a natural tendency, especially on the part of the generation which grew up during the Cold War, to take a fresh look at the causes of the great contention between Russia and America.

Some exercises in reappraisal have merely elaborated the orthodoxies promulgated in Washington or Moscow during the boom years of the Cold War. But others, especially in the United States (there are no signs, alas, of this in the Soviet Union), represent what American historians call "revisionism"—that is, a readiness to challenge official explanations. No one should be surprised by this phenomenon. Every war in American history has been followed in due course by skeptical reassessments of supposedly sacred assumptions. So the War of 1812, fought at the time for the freedom of the seas, was in later years ascribed to the expansionist ambitions of Congressional war hawks; so the Mexican War became a slaveholders' conspiracy. So the Civil War has been pronounced a "needless war," and Lincoln has even been accused of manœuvring the rebel attack on Fort Sumter. So too the Spanish-American War and the First and Second World Wars have, each in its turn, undergone revisionist critiques. It is not to be supposed that the Cold War would remain exempt.

In the case of the Cold War, special factors reinforce the predictable historiographical rhythm. The outburst of polycentrism in the Communist empire has made people wonder whether communism was ever so monolithic as official theories of the Cold War supposed. A generation with no vivid memories of Stalinism may see the Russia of the forties in the image of the relatively mild, seedy, and irresolute Russia of the sixties. And for this same generation the American course of widening the war in Vietnam—which even nonrevisionists can easily regard as folly —has unquestionably stirred doubts about the wisdom of American foreign policy in the sixties which younger historians may have begun to read back into the forties.

It is useful to remember that, on the whole, past exercises in revisionism have failed to stick. Few historians today believe that the war hawks caused the War of 1812 or the slaveholders the Mexican War, or that the Civil War was needless, or that the House of Morgan brought America into the First World War or that Franklin Roosevelt schemed to produce the attack on

Pearl Harbor. But this does not mean that one should deplore the rise of Cold War revisionism.[1] For revisionism is an essential part of the process by which history, through the posing of new problems and the investigation of new possibilities, enlarges its perspectives and enriches its insights.

More than this, in the present context, revisionism expresses a deep, legitimate, and tragic apprehension. As the Cold War has begun to lose its purity of definition, as the moral absolutes of the fifties become the moralistic clichés of the sixties, some have begun to ask whether the appalling risks which humanity ran during the Cold War were, after all, necessary and inevitable, whether more restrained and rational policies might not have guided the energies of man from the perils of conflict into the potentialities of collaboration. The fact that such questions are in their nature unanswerable does not mean that it is not right and useful to raise them. Nor does it mean that our sons and daughters are not entitled to an accounting from the generation of Russians and Americans who produced the Cold War.

The orthodox American view, as originally set forth by the American government and as reaffirmed until recently by most American scholars, has been that the Cold War was the brave and essential response of free men to communist aggression. Some have gone back well before the Second World War to lay open the sources of Russian expansionism. Geopoliticians traced the Cold War to imperial Russian strategic ambitions which in the nineteenth century led to the Crimean War, to Russian penetration of the Balkans and the Middle East, and to Russian pressure on Britain's "lifeline" to India. Ideologists traced it to the Communist Manifesto of 1848 ("the violent overthrow of the bourgeoisie lays the foundation for the sway of the proletariat"). Thoughtful observers (a phrase meant to exclude those who speak in Dullese about the unlimited evil of godless, atheistic, militant communism) concluded that classical Russian imperialism

---

[1] As this writer somewhat intemperately did in a letter to *The New York Review of Books,* October 20, 1966.

and Pan-Slavism, compounded after 1917 by Leninist messianism, confronted the West at the end of the Second World War with an inexorable drive for domination.[2]

The revisionist thesis is very different.[3] In its extreme form, it is that, after the death of Franklin Roosevelt and the end of the Second World War, the United States deliberately abandoned the wartime policy of collaboration and, exhilarated by the possession of the atomic bomb, undertook a course of aggression of its own designed to expel all Russian influence from Eastern Europe and to establish democratic-capitalist states on the very border of the Soviet Union. As the revisionists see it, this radically new American policy—or rather this resumption by Tru-

---

[2] Every student of the Cold War must acknowledge his debt to W. H. McNeill's remarkable account, *America, Britain and Russia: Their Cooperation and Conflict, 1941–1946* (New York: Oxford University Press, 1953) and to the brilliant and indispensable series by Herbert Feis: *Churchill, Roosevelt, Stalin: The War They Waged and the Peace They Sought* (Princeton: Princeton University Press, 1957); *Between War and Peace: The Potsdam Conference* (Princeton: Princeton University Press, 1960); and *The Atomic Bomb and the End of World War II* (Princeton: Princeton University Press, 1966). Useful recent analyses include André Fontaine, *Histoire de la Guerre Froide* (2 v., Paris, 1965, 1967); N. A. Graebner, *Cold War Diplomacy, 1945–1960* (Princeton: Van Nostrand, 1962); L. J. Halle, *The Cold War as History* (London: Chatto & Windus, 1967); M. F. Herz, *Beginnings of the Cold War* (Bloomington: Indiana University Press, 1966) and W. L. Neumann, *After Victory: Churchill, Roosevelt, Stalin and the Making of the Peace* (New York: Oxford University Press, 1967).

[3] The fullest statement of this case is to be found in D. F. Fleming's voluminous *The Cold War and Its Origins* (New York: Doubleday, 1961). For a shorter version of this argument, see David Horowitz, *The Free World Colossus* (New York: Hill and Wang, 1965); the most subtle and ingenious statements come in W. A. Williams' *The Tragedy of American Diplomacy* (rev. ed., New York: Dell, 1962) and in Gar Alperovitz's *Atomic Diplomacy: Hiroshima and Potsdam* (New York: Simon & Schuster, 1965) and in subsequent articles and reviews by Mr. Alperovitz in *The New York Review of Books.* The fact that in some aspects the revisionist thesis parallels the official Soviet argument must not, of course, prevent consideration of the case on its merits, nor raise questions about the motives of the writers, all of whom, so far as I know, are independent-minded scholars.

I might further add that all these books, in spite of their ostentatious display of scholarly apparatus, must be used with caution. Professor Fleming, for example, relies heavily on newspaper articles and even columnists. While Mr. Alperovitz bases his case on official documents or authoritative remi-

man of the pre-Roosevelt policy of insensate anti-communism—left Moscow no alternative but to take measures in defense of its own borders. The result was the Cold War.

These two views, of course, could not be more starkly contrasting. It is therefore not unreasonable to look again at the half-dozen critical years between June 22, 1941, when Hitler attacked Russia, and July 2, 1947, when the Russians walked out of the Marshall Plan meeting in Paris. Several things should be borne in mind as this reexamination is made. For one thing, we have thought a great deal more in recent years, in part because of writers like Roberta Wohlstetter and T. C. Schelling, about the problems of communication in diplomacy—the signals which one nation, by word or by deed, gives, inadvertently or intentionally, to another. Any honest reappraisal of the origins of the Cold War requires the imaginative leap—which should in any case be as instinctive for the historian as it is prudent for the statesman—into the adversary's viewpoint. We must strive to see how, given Soviet perspectives, the Russians might conceivably

niscences, he sometimes twists his material in a most unscholarly way. For example, in describing Ambassador Harriman's talk with President Truman on April 20, 1945, Mr. Alperovitz writes: "He argued that a reconsideration of Roosevelt's policy was necessary" (p. 22, repeated on p. 24). The citation is to p. 70–72 in President Truman's *Years of Decision.* What President Truman reported Harriman as saying was the exact opposite: "Before leaving, Harriman took me aside and said, 'Frankly, one of the reasons that made me rush back to Washington was the fear that you did not understand, as I had seen Roosevelt understand, that Stalin is breaking his agreements.' " Similarly, in an appendix (p. 271) Mr. Alperovitz writes that the Hopkins and Davies missions of May 1945 "were opposed by the 'firm' advisers." Actually the Hopkins mission was proposed by Harriman and Charles E. Bohlen, who Mr. Alperovitz elsewhere suggests were the firmest of the firm—and was proposed by them precisely to impress on Stalin the continuity of American policy from Roosevelt to Truman. While the idea that Truman reversed Roosevelt's policy is tempting dramatically, it is a myth. See, for example, the testimony of Anna Rosenberg Hoffman, who lunched with Roosevelt on March 24, 1945, the last day he spent in Washington. After luncheon, Roosevelt was handed a cable. "He read it and became quite angry. He banged his fists on the arms of his wheelchair and said, 'Averell is right; we can't do business with Stalin. He has broken every one of the promises he made at Yalta.' He was very upset and continued in the same vein on the subject."

have misread our signals, as we must reconsider how intelligently we read theirs.

For another, the historian must not overindulge the man of power in the illusion cherished by those in office that high position carries with it the easy ability to shape history. Violating the statesman's creed, Lincoln once blurted out the truth in his letter of 1864 to A. G. Hodges: "I claim not to have controlled events, but confess plainly that events have controlled me." He was not asserting Tolstoyan fatalism but rather suggesting how greatly events limit the capacity of the statesman to bend history to his will. The physical course of the Second World War—the military operations undertaken, the position of the respective armies at the war's end, the momentum generated by victory, and the vacuums created by defeat—all these determined the future as much as the character of individual leaders and the substance of national ideology and purpose.

Nor can the historian forget the conditions under which decisions are made, especially in a time like the Second World War. These were tired, overworked, aging men: in 1945, Churchill was 71 years old, Stalin had governed his country for 17 exacting years, Roosevelt his for 12 years nearly as exacting. During the war, moreover, the importunities of military operations had shoved postwar questions to the margins of their minds. All—even Stalin, behind his screen of ideology—had become addicts of improvisation, relying on authority and virtuosity to conceal the fact that they were constantly surprised by developments. Like Eliza, they leaped from one cake of ice to the next in the effort to reach the other side of the river. None showed great tactical consistency, or cared much about it; all employed a certain ambiguity to preserve their power to decide big issues; and it is hard to know how to interpret anything any one of them said on any specific occasion. This was partly because, like all princes, they designed their expressions to have particular effects on particular audiences; partly because the entirely genuine intellectual difficulty of the questions they faced made a degree of vacillation and mind-changing eminently reasonable. If historians cannot solve their problems in retrospect, who are they to blame Roosevelt, Stalin, and Churchill for not having solved them at the time?

Peacemaking after the Second World War was not so much a tapestry as it was a hopelessly raveled and knotted mess of yarn. Yet, for purposes of clarity, it is essential to follow certain threads. One theme indispensable to an understanding of the Cold War is the contrast between two clashing views of world order: the "universalist" view, by which all nations shared a common interest in all the affairs of the world, and the "sphere-of-influence" view, by which each great power would be assured by the other great powers of an acknowledged predominance in its own area of special interest. The universalist view assumed that national security would be guaranteed by an international organization. The sphere-of-interest view assumed that national security would be guaranteed by the balance of power. While in practice these views have by no means been incompatible (indeed, our shaky peace has been based on a combination of the two), in the abstract they involved sharp contradictions.

The tradition of American thought in these matters was universalist—that is, Wilsonian. Roosevelt had been a member of Wilson's subcabinet; in 1920, as candidate for Vice-President, he had campaigned for the League of Nations. It is true that, within Roosevelt's infinitely complex mind, Wilsonianism warred with the perception of vital strategic interests he had imbibed from Mahan. Moreover, his temperamental inclination to settle things with fellow princes around the conference table led him to regard the Big Three—or Four—as trustees for the rest of the world. On occasion, as this narrative will show, he was beguiled into flirtation with the sphere-of-influence heresy. But in principle he believed in joint action and remained a Wilsonian. His hope for Yalta, as he told the Congress on his return, was that it would "spell the end of the system of unilateral action, the exclusive alliances, the spheres of influence, the balances of power, and all the other expedients that have been tried for centuries—and have always failed."

Whenever Roosevelt backslid, he had at his side that Wilsonian fundamentalist, Secretary of State Cordell Hull, to recall him to the pure faith. After his visit to Moscow in 1943, Hull characteristically said that, with the Declaration of Four Nations on General Security (in which America, Russia, Britain, and China pledged "united action . . . for the organization and maintenance of peace and security"), "there will no longer be need for spheres of influence, for alliances, for balance of power, or any other of the special arrangements through which, in the unhappy past, the nations strove to safeguard their security or to promote their interests."

Remembering the corruption of the Wilsonian vision by the secret treaties of the First World War, Hull was determined to prevent any sphere-of-influence nonsense after the Second World War. He therefore fought all proposals to settle border questions while the war was still on and, excluded as he largely was from wartime diplomacy, poured his not inconsiderable moral energy and frustration into the promulgation of virtuous and spacious general principles.

In adopting the universalist view, Roosevelt and Hull were not indulging personal hobbies. Sumner Welles, Adolf Berle, Averell Harriman, Charles Bohlen—all, if with a variety of nuances, opposed the sphere-of-influence approach. And here the State Department was expressing what seems clearly to have been the predominant mood of the American people, so long mistrustful of European power politics. The Republicans shared the true faith. John Foster Dulles argued that the great threat to peace after the war would lie in the revival of sphere-of-influence thinking. The United States, he said, must not permit Britain and Russia to revert to these bad old ways; it must therefore insist on American participation in all policy decisions for all territories in the world. Dulles wrote pessimistically in January 1945, "The three great powers which at Moscow agreed upon the 'closest cooperation' about European questions have shifted to a practice of separate, regional responsibility."

It is true that critics, and even friends, of the United States sometimes noted a discrepancy between the American passion for universalism when it applied to territory far from American shores and the preeminence the United States accorded its own interests nearer home. Churchill, seeking Washington's blessing for a sphere-of-influence initiative in Eastern Europe, could not forbear reminding the Americans, "We follow the lead of the United States in South America;" nor did any universalist of record propose the abolition of the Monroe Doctrine. But a convenient myopia prevented such inconsistencies from qualifying the ardency of the universalist faith.

There seem only to have been three officials in the United States Government who dissented. One was the Secretary of War, Henry L. Stimson, a classical balance-of-power man, who in 1944 opposed the creation of a vacuum in Central Europe by the pastoralization of Germany and in 1945 urged "the settlement of all territorial acquisitions in the shape of defense posts which each of these four powers may deem to be necessary for their own safety" in advance of any effort to establish a peacetime United Nations. Stimson considered the claim of Russia to a preferred position in Eastern Europe as not unreasonable: as he told President Truman, he "thought the Russians perhaps were being more realistic than we were in regard to their own security." Such a position for Russia seemed to him comparable to the preferred American position in Latin America; he even spoke of "our respective orbits." Stimson was therefore skeptical of what he regarded as the prevailing tendency "to hang on to exaggerated views of the Monroe Doctrine and at the same time butt into every question that comes up in Central Europe." Acceptance of spheres of influence seemed to him the way to avoid "a head-on collision."

A second official opponent of universalism was George Kennan, an eloquent advocate from the American Embassy in Moscow of "a prompt and clear recognition of the division of Europe into spheres of influence and of a policy based on the fact of such division." Kennan argued that nothing we could do would possibly alter the course of events in Eastern Europe; that we were deceiving ourselves by supposing that these countries had any future but Russian domination; that we should therefore relinquish Eastern Europe to the Soviet Union and avoid anything which would make things easier for the Russians by giving them economic assistance or by sharing moral responsibility for their actions.

A third voice within the government against universalism was (at least after the war) Henry A. Wallace. As Secretary of Commerce, he stated the sphere-of-influence case with trenchancy in the famous Madison Square Garden speech of September 1946 which led to his dismissal by President Truman:

> On our part, we should recognize that we have no more business in the *political* affairs of Eastern Europe than Russia has in the *political* affairs of Latin America, Western Europe, and the United States. . . . Whether we like it or not, the Russians will try to socialize their sphere of influence just as we try to democratize our sphere of influence. . . . The Russians have no more business stirring up native Communists to political activity in Western Europe, Latin America, and the United States than we have in interfering with the politics of Eastern Europe and Russia.

Stimson, Kennan, and Wallace seem to have been alone in the government, however, in taking these views. They were very much minority voices. Meanwhile universalism, rooted in the American legal and moral tradition, overwhelmingly backed by contemporary opinion, received successive enshrinements in the Atlantic Charter of 1941, in the Declaration of the United Nations in 1942, and in the Moscow Declaration of 1943.

The Kremlin, on the other hand, thought *only* of spheres of interest; above all, the Russians were determined to protect their frontiers, and especially their border to the west, crossed so often and so bloodily in the dark course of their history. These western frontiers lacked natural means of defense—no great oceans, rugged mountains, steaming swamps, or impenetrable jungles. The history of Russia had been the history of invasion, the last of which was by now horribly killing up to twenty million of its people. The protocol of Russia therefore meant the enlargement of the area of Russian influence. Kennan himself wrote (in May 1944), "Behind Russia's stubborn expansion lies only the age-old sense of insecurity of a sedentary people reared on an exposed plain in the neighborhood of fierce nomadic peoples," and he called this "urge" a "permanent feature of Russian psychology."

In earlier times the "urge" had produced the tsarist search for buffer states and maritime outlets. In 1939 the Soviet-Nazi pact and its secret protocol had enabled Russia to begin to satisfy in the Baltic states, Karelian Finland and Poland, part of what it conceived as its security requirements in Eastern Europe. But the "urge" persisted, causing the friction between Russia and Germany in 1940 as each jostled for position in the area which separated them. Later it led to Molotov's new demands on Hitler in November 1940—a free hand in Finland, Soviet predominance in Rumania and Bulgaria, bases in the Dardanelles—the demands which convinced Hitler that he had no choice but to attack Russia. Now Stalin hoped to gain from the West what Hitler, a closer neighbor, had not dared yield him.

It is true that, so long as Russian survival appeared to require a second front to relieve the Nazi pressure, Moscow's demand for Eastern Europe was a little muffled. Thus the Soviet government adhered to the Atlantic Charter (though with a significant if obscure reservation about adapting its principles to "the circumstances, needs, and historic peculiarities of particular countries"). Thus it also adhered to the Moscow Declaration of 1943, and Molotov then, with his easy mendacity, even denied that Russia had any desire to divide Europe into spheres of influence. But this was guff, which the Russians were perfectly willing to ladle out if it would keep the Americans, and especially Secretary Hull (who made a strong personal impression at the Moscow conference) happy. "A declaration," as Stalin once observed to Eden, "I regard as algebra, but an agreement as practical arithmetic. I do not wish to decry algebra, but I prefer practical arithmetic."

The more consistent Russian purpose was revealed when Stalin offered the British a straight sphere-of-influence deal at the end of 1941. Britain, he suggested, should recognize the Russian absorption of the Baltic states, part of Finland, eastern Poland, and Bessarabia; in return, Russia would support any special British need for bases or security arrangements in Western Europe. There was nothing specifically Communist about these ambitions.

If Stalin achieved them, he would be fulfilling an age-old dream of the tsars. The British reaction was mixed. "Soviet policy is amoral," as Anthony Eden noted at the time; "United States policy is exaggeratedly moral, at least where non-American interests are concerned." If Roosevelt was a universalist with occasional leanings toward spheres of influence and Stalin was a sphere-of-influence man with occasional gestures toward universalism, Churchill seemed evenly poised between the familiar realism of the balance of power, which he had so long recorded as an historian and manipulated as a statesman, and the hope that there must be some better way of doing things. His 1943 proposal of a world organization divided into regional councils represented an effort to blend universalist and sphere-of-interest conceptions. His initial rejection of Stalin's proposal in December 1941 as "directly contrary to the first, second, and third articles of the Atlantic Charter" thus did not spring entirely from a desire to propitiate the United States. On the other hand, he had himself already reinterpreted the Atlantic Charter as applying only to Europe (and thus not to the British Empire), and he was, above all, an empiricist who never believed in sacrificing reality on the altar of doctrine.

So in April 1942 he wrote Roosevelt that "the increasing gravity of the war" had led him to feel that the Charter "ought not to be construed so as to deny Russia the frontiers she occupied when Germany attacked her." Hull, however, remained fiercely hostile to the inclusion of territorial provisions in the Anglo-Russian treaty; the American position, Eden noted, "chilled me with Wilsonian memories." Though Stalin complained that it looked "as if the Atlantic Charter was directed against the U.S.S.R.," it was the Russian season of military adversity in the spring of 1942, and he dropped his demands.

He did not, however, change his intentions. A year later Ambassador Standley could cable Washington from Moscow: "In 1918 Western Europe attempted to set up a *cordon sanitaire* to protect it from the influence of bolshevism. Might not now the Kremlin envisage the formation of a belt of pro-Soviet states to protect it from the influences of the West?" It well might; and that purpose became increasingly clear as the war approached its end. Indeed, it derived sustenance from Western policy in the first area of liberation.

The unconditional surrender of Italy in July 1943 created the first major test of the Western devotion to universalism. America and Britain, having won the Italian war, handled the capitulation, keeping Moscow informed at a distance. Stalin complained:

> The United States and Great Britain made agreements but the Soviet Union received information about the results . . . just as a passive third observer. I have to tell you that it is impossible to tolerate the situation any longer. I propose that the [tripartite military-political commission] be established and that Sicily be assigned . . . as its place of residence.

Roosevelt, who had no intention of sharing the control of Italy with the Russians, suavely replied with the suggestion that Stalin send an officer "to General Eisenhower's headquarters in connection with the commission." Unimpressed, Stalin continued to press for a tripartite body; but his Western allies were adamant in keeping the Soviet Union off the Control Commission for Italy, and the Russians in the end had to be satisfied with a seat, along with minor Allied states, on a meaningless Inter-Allied Advisory Council. Their acquiescence in this was doubtless not unconnected with a desire to establish precedents for Eastern Europe.

Teheran in December 1943 marked the high point of three-power collaboration. Still, when Churchill asked about Russian territorial interests, Stalin replied a little ominously, "There is no need to speak at the present time about any Soviet desires, but when the time comes we will speak." In the next weeks, there were increasing indications of a Soviet determination to deal unilaterally with Eastern Europe—so much so that in early February 1944 Hull cabled Harriman in Moscow:

> Matters are rapidly approaching the point where the Soviet Government will have to choose between the development and extension of the foundation of international cooperation as the guiding principle of the postwar world as against the continuance

of a unilateral and arbitrary method of dealing with its special problems even though these problems are admittedly of more direct interest to the Soviet Union than to other great powers.

As against this approach, however, Churchill, more tolerant of sphere-of-influence deviations, soon proposed that, with the impending liberation of the Balkans, Russia should run things in Rumania and Britain in Greece. Hull strongly opposed this suggestion but made the mistake of leaving Washington for a few days; and Roosevelt, momentarily free from his Wilsonian conscience, yielded to Churchill's plea for a three-months' trial. Hull resumed the fight on his return, and Churchill postponed the matter.

The Red Army continued its advance into Eastern Europe. In August the Polish Home Army, urged on by Polish-language broadcasts from Moscow, rose up against the Nazis in Warsaw. For 63 terrible days, the Poles fought valiantly on, while the Red Army halted on the banks of the Vistula a few miles away, and in Moscow Stalin for more than half this time declined to cooperate with the Western effort to drop supplies to the Warsaw Resistance. It appeared a calculated Soviet decision to let the Nazis slaughter the anti-Soviet Polish underground; and, indeed, the result was to destroy any substantial alternative to a Soviet solution in Poland. The agony of Warsaw caused the most deep and genuine moral shock in Britain and America and provoked dark forebodings about Soviet postwar purposes.

Again history enjoins the imaginative leap in order to see things for a moment from Moscow's viewpoint. The Polish question, Churchill would say at Yalta, was for Britain a question of honor. "It is not only a question of honor for Russia," Stalin replied, "but one of life and death. . . . Throughout history Poland had been the corridor for attack on Russia." A top postwar priority for any Russian regime must be to close that corridor. The Home Army was led by anti-Communists. It clearly hoped by its action to forestall the Soviet occupation of Warsaw and, in Russian eyes, to prepare the way for an anti-Russian Poland. In addition, the uprising from a strictly operational viewpoint was premature.

The Russians, it is evident in retrospect, had real military problems at the Vistula. The Soviet attempt in September to send Polish units from the Red Army across the river to join forces with the Home Army was a disaster. Heavy German shelling thereafter prevented the ferrying of tanks necessary for an assault on the German position. The Red Army itself did not take Warsaw for another three months. Nonetheless, Stalin's indifference to the human tragedy, his effort to blackmail the London Poles during the ordeal, his sanctimonious opposition during five precious weeks to aerial resupply, the invariable coldness of his explanations ("the Soviet command has come to the conclusion that it must dissociate itself from the Warsaw adventure"), and the obvious political benefit to the Soviet Union from the destruction of the Home Army—all these had the effect of suddenly dropping the mask of wartime comradeship and displaying to the West the hard face of Soviet policy. In now pursuing what he grimly regarded as the minimal requirements for the postwar security of his country, Stalin was inadvertently showing the irreconcilability of both his means and his ends with the Anglo-American conception of the peace.

Meanwhile Eastern Europe presented the Alliance with still another crisis that same September. Bulgaria, which was not at war with Russia, decided to surrender to the Western Allies while it still could; and the English and Americans at Cairo began to discuss armistice terms with Bulgarian envoys. Moscow, challenged by what it plainly saw as a Western intrusion into its own zone of vital interest, promptly declared war on Bulgaria, took over the surrender negotiations and, invoking the Italian precedent, denied its Western Allies any role in the Bulgarian Control Commission. In a long and thoughtful cable, Ambassador Harriman meditated on the problems of communication with the Soviet Union. "Words," he reflected," have a different connotation to the Soviets than they have to us. When they speak of insisting on 'friendly governments' in their neighboring countries, they have in mind something quite different from what we would mean." The Russians, he surmised, really believed that Washington accepted "their position that although they would keep us informed they had the right to settle their problems with their western neighbors unilaterally." But the Soviet position was still in flux: "the Soviet Government is not one mind." The problem, as Harriman had earlier told Harry Hopkins, was "to strengthen the hands of those around Stalin who want to play the game along our lines." The way to do this, he now told Hull, was to

> be understanding of their sensitivity, meet them much more than half way, encourage them and support them wherever we can, and yet oppose them promptly with the greatest of firmness where we see them going wrong. . . . The only way we can eventually come to an understanding with the Soviet Union on the question of non-interference in the internal affairs of other countries is for us to take a definite interest in the solution of the problems of each individual country as they arise.

As against Harriman's sophisticated universalist strategy, however, Churchill, increasingly fearful of the consequences of unrestrained competition in Eastern Europe, decided in early October to carry his sphere-of-influence proposal directly to Moscow. Roosevelt was at first content to have Churchill speak for him too and even prepared a cable to that effect. But Hopkins, a more rigorous universalist, took it upon himself to stop the cable and warn Roosevelt of its possible implications. Eventually Roosevelt sent a message to Harriman in Moscow emphasizing that he expected to "retain complete freedom of action after this conference is over." It was now that Churchill quickly proposed—and Stalin as quickly accepted—the celebrated division of southeastern Europe: ending (after further haggling between Eden and Molotov) with 90 per cent Soviet predominance in Rumania, 80 per cent in Bulgaria and Hungary, fifty-fifty in Jugoslavia, 90 per cent British predominance in Greece.

Churchill in discussing this with Harriman used the phrase "spheres of influence." But he insisted that these were only "immediate wartime arrangements" and received a highly general blessing from Roosevelt. Yet, whatever Churchill intended, there is reason to believe that Stalin construed the percentages as an agreement, not a declaration, as practical arithmetic, not algebra.

For Stalin, it should be understood, the sphere-of-influence idea did not mean that he would abandon all efforts to spread communism in some other nation's sphere; it did mean that, if he tried this and the other side cracked down, he could not feel he had serious cause for complaint. As Kennan wrote to Harriman at the end of 1944:

> As far as border states are concerned the Soviet government has never ceased to think in terms of spheres of interest. They expect us to support them in whatever action they wish to take in those regions, regardless of whether that action seems to us or to the rest of the world to be right or wrong. . . . I have no doubt that this position is honestly maintained on their part, and that they would be equally prepared to reserve moral judgment on any actions which we might wish to carry out, i.e., in the Caribbean area.

In any case, the matter was already under test a good deal closer to Moscow than the Caribbean. The Communist-dominated resistance movement in Greece was in open revolt against the effort of the Papandreou government to disarm and disband the guerrillas (the same Papandreou whom the Greek colonels have recently arrested on the claim that he is a tool of the Communists). Churchill now called in British Army units to crush the insurrection. This action produced a storm of criticism in his own country and in the United States; the American Government even publicly dissociated itself from the intervention, thereby emphasizing its detachment from the sphere-of-influence deal. But Stalin, Churchill later claimed, "adhered strictly and faithfully to our agreement of October, and during all the long weeks of fighting the Communists in the streets of Athens not one word of reproach came from *Pravda* or *Izvestia*," though there is no evidence that he tried to call off the Greek Communists. Still, when the Communist rebellion later broke out again in Greece, Stalin told Kardelj and Djilas of Jugoslavia in 1948, "The uprising in Greece must be stopped, and as quickly as possible."

No one, of course, can know what really was in the minds of the Russian leaders. The Kremlin archives are locked; of the primary actors, only Molotov survives, and he has not yet indicated any desire to collaborate with the Columbia Oral History Project. We do know that Stalin did not wholly surrender to sentimental illusion about his new friends. In June 1944, on the night before the landings in Normandy, he told Djilas that the English "find nothing sweeter than to trick their allies. . . . And Churchill? Churchill is the kind who, if you don't watch him, will slip a kopeck out of your pocket. Yes, a kopeck out of your pocket! . . . Roosevelt is not like that. He dips in his hand only for bigger coins." But whatever his views of his colleagues it is not unreasonable to suppose that Stalin would have been satisfied at the end of the war to secure what Kennan has called "a protective glacis along Russia's western border," and that, in exchange for a free hand in Eastern Europe, he was prepared to give the British and Americans equally free hands in their zones of vital interest, including in nations as close to Russia as Greece (for the British) and, very probably—or at least so the Jugoslavs believe—China (for the United States). In other words, his initial objectives were very probably not world conquest but Russian security.

It is now pertinent to inquire why the United States rejected the idea of stabilizing the world by division into spheres of influence and insisted on an East European strategy. One should warn against rushing to the conclusion that it was all a row between hard-nosed, balance-of-power realists and starry-eyed Wilsonians. Roosevelt, Hopkins, Welles, Harriman, Bohlen, Berle, Dulles, and other universalists were tough and serious men. Why then did they rebuff the sphere-of-influence solution?

The first reason is that they regarded this solution as containing within itself the seeds of a third world war. The balance-of-power idea seemed inherently unstable. It had always broken down in the past. It held out to each power the permanent temptation to try to alter the balance in its own favor, and it built this temptation into the international order. It would turn the great powers of 1945 away from the objective of concerting common policies toward competition for postwar advantage. As Hopkins told

Molotov at Teheran, "The President feels it essential to world peace that Russia, Great Britain, and the United States work out this control question in a manner which will not start each of the three powers arming against the others." "The greatest likelihood of eventual conflict," said the Joint Chiefs of Staff in 1944 (the only conflict which the J.C.S., in its wisdom, could then glimpse "in the foreseeable future" was between Britain and Russia), ". . . would seem to grow out of either nation initiating attempts to build up its strength, by seeking to attach to herself parts of Europe to the disadvantage and possible danger of her potential adversary." The Americans were perfectly ready to acknowledge that Russia was entitled to convincing assurance of her national security—but not this way. "I could sympathize fully with Stalin's desire to protect his western borders from future attack," as Hull put it. "But I felt that this security could best be obtained through a strong postwar peace organization."

Hull's remark suggests the second objection: that the sphere-of-influence approach would, in the words of the State Department in 1945, "militate against the establishment and effective functioning of a broader system of general security in which all countries will have their part." The United Nations, in short, was seen as the alternative to the balance of power. Nor did the universalists see any necessary incompatibility between the Russian desire for "friendly governments" on its frontier and the American desire for self-determination in Eastern Europe. Before Yalta the State Department judged the general mood of Europe as "to the left and strongly in favor of far-reaching economic and social reforms, but not, however, in favor of a left-wing totalitarian regime to achieve these reforms." Governments in Eastern Europe could be sufficiently to the left "to allay Soviet suspicions" but sufficiently representative "of the center and *petit bourgeois* elements" not to seem a prelude to communist dictatorship. The American criteria were therefore that the government "should be dedicated to the preservation of civil liberties" and "should favor social and economic reforms." A string of New Deal states—of Finlands and Czechoslovakias—seemed a reasonable compromise solution.

Third, the universalists feared that the sphere-of-interest approach would be what Hull termed "a haven for the isolationists," who would advocate America's participation in Western Hemisphere affairs on condition that it did not participate in European or Asian affairs. Hull also feared that spheres of interest would lead to "closed trade areas or discriminatory systems" and thus defeat his cherished dream of a low-tariff, freely trading world.

Fourth, the sphere-of-interest solution meant the betrayal of the principles for which the Second World War was being fought—the Atlantic Charter, the Four Freedoms, the Declaration of the United Nations. Poland summed up the problem. Britain, having gone to war to defend the independence of Poland from the Germans, could not easily conclude the war by surrendering the independence of Poland to the Russians. Thus, as Hopkins told Stalin after Roosevelt's death in 1945, Poland had "become the symbol of our ability to work out problems with the Soviet Union." Nor could American liberals in general watch with equanimity while the police state spread into countries which, if they had mostly not been real democracies, had mostly not been tyrannies either. The execution in 1943 of Ehrlich and Alter, the Polish socialist trade union leaders, excited deep concern. "I have particularly in mind," Harriman cabled in 1944, "objection to the institution of secret police who may become involved in the persecution of persons of truly democratic convictions who may not be willing to conform to Soviet methods."

Fifth, the sphere-of-influence solution would create difficult domestic problems in American politics. Roosevelt was aware of the six million or more Polish votes in the 1944 election; even more acutely, he was aware of the broader and deeper attack which would follow if, after going to war to stop the Nazi conquest of Europe, he permitted the war to end with the Communist conquest of Eastern Europe. As Archibald MacLeish, then Assistant Secretary of State for Public Affairs, warned in January 1945, "The wave of disillusionment which has distressed us in the last several weeks will be increased if the impression is permitted to get abroad that potentially totalitarian provisional governments are to be set up without adequate safeguards as to the holding of free elections and the realization of the principles of the Atlantic Charter." Roosevelt believed that no administration could survive which did not try everything short of war to save Eastern Europe, and he was the supreme American politician of the century.

Sixth, if the Russians were allowed to overrun Eastern Europe without argument, would that satisfy them? Even Kennan, in a dispatch of May 1944, admitted that the "urge" had dreadful potentialities: "If initially successful, will it know where to stop? Will it not be inexorably carried forward, by its very nature, in a struggle to reach the whole—to attain complete mastery of the shores of the Atlantic and the Pacific?" His own answer was that there were inherent limits to the Russian capacity to expand— "that Russia will not have an easy time in maintaining the power which it has seized over other people in Eastern and Central Europe, unless it receives both moral and material assistance from the West." Subsequent developments have vindicated Kennan's argument. By the late forties, Jugoslavia and Albania, the two East European states farthest from the Soviet Union and the two in which communism was imposed from within rather than from without, had declared their independence of Moscow. But, given Russia's success in maintaining centralized control over the international Communist movement for a quarter of a century, who in 1944 could have had much confidence in the idea of Communist revolts against Moscow?

Most of those involved therefore rejected Kennan's answer and stayed with his question. If the West turned its back on Eastern Europe, the higher probability, in their view, was that the Russians would use their security zone, not just for defensive purposes, but as a springboard from which to mount an attack on Western Europe, now shattered by war, a vacuum of power awaiting its master. "If the policy is accepted that the Soviet Union has a right to penetrate her immediate neighbors for security," Harriman said in 1944, "penetration of the next immediate neighbors becomes at a certain time equally logical." If a row with Russia were inevitable, every consideration of prudence dictated that it should take place in Eastern rather than Western Europe.

Thus idealism and realism joined in opposition to the sphere-of-influence solution. The consequence was a determination to assert an American interest in the postwar destiny of all nations, including those of Eastern Europe. In the message which Roosevelt and Hopkins drafted after Hopkins had stopped Roosevelt's initial cable authorizing Churchill to speak for the United States at the Moscow meeting of October 1944, Roosevelt now said, "There is in this global war literally no question, either military or political, in which the United States is not interested." After Roosevelt's death Hopkins repeated the point to Stalin: "The cardinal basis of President Roosevelt's policy which the American people had fully supported had been the concept that the interests of the U.S. were worldwide and not confined to North and South America and the Pacific Ocean."

For better or worse, this was the American position. It is now necessary to attempt the imaginative leap and consider the impact of this position on the leaders of the Soviet Union who, also for better or for worse, had reached the bitter conclusion that the survival of their country depended on their unchallenged control of the corridors through which enemies had so often invaded their homeland. They could claim to have been keeping their own side of the sphere-of-influence bargain. Of course, they were working to capture the resistance movements of Western Europe; indeed, with the appointment of Oumansky as Ambassador to Mexico they were even beginning to enlarge underground operations in the Western Hemisphere. But, from their viewpoint, if the West permitted this, the more fools they; and, if the West stopped it, it was within their right to do so. In overt political matters the Russians were scrupulously playing the game. They had watched in silence while the British shot down Communists in Greece. In Jugoslavia Stalin was urging Tito (as Djilas later revealed) to keep King Peter. They had not only acknowledged Western preeminence in Italy but had recognized the Badoglio regime; the Italian Communists had even voted (against the Socialists and the Liberals) for the renewal of the Lateran Pacts.

They would not regard anti-Communist action in a Western zone as a *casus belli;* and they expected reciprocal license to assert their own authority in the East. But the principle of self-determination was carrying the United States into a deeper entanglement in Eastern Europe than the Soviet Union claimed as a right (whatever it was doing underground) in the affairs of Italy, Greece or China. When the Russians now exercised in Eastern Europe the same brutal control they were prepared to have Washington exercise in the American sphere of influence, the American protests, given the paranoia produced alike by Russian history and Leninist ideology, no doubt seemed not only an act of hypocrisy but a threat to security. To the Russians, a stroll into the neighborhood easily became a plot to burn down the house: when, for example, damaged American planes made emergency landings in Poland and Hungary, Moscow took this as attempts to organize the local resistance. It is not unusual to suspect one's adversary of doing what one is already doing oneself. At the same time, the cruelty with which the Russians executed their idea of spheres of influence—in a sense, perhaps, an unwitting cruelty, since Stalin treated the East Europeans no worse than he had treated the Russians in the thirties—discouraged the West from accepting the equation (for example, Italy = Rumania) which seemed so self-evident to the Kremlin.

So Moscow very probably, and not unnaturally, perceived the emphasis on self-determination as a systematic and deliberate pressure on Russia's western frontiers. Moreover, the restoration of capitalism to countries freed at frightful cost by the Red Army no doubt struck the Russians as the betrayal of the principles for which *they* were fighting. "That they, the victors," Isaac Deutscher has suggested, "should now preserve an order from which they had experienced nothing but hostility, and could expect nothing but hostility . . . would have been the most miserable anti-climax to their great 'war of liberation.' " By 1944 Poland was the critical issue; Harriman later said that "under instructions from President Roosevelt, I talked about Poland with Stalin more frequently than any other subject." While the West saw the point of Stalin's demand for a "friendly government" in Warsaw, the American insistence on the sovereign virtues of free elections (ironically in the spirit of the 1917 bolshevik decree of peace, which affirmed "the right" of a nation "to decide the forms of its state existence by a free vote, taken after the complete evacuation of the incorporating or, generally, of the stronger nation") created an insoluble problem in those countries, like Poland (and Rumania) where free elections would almost certainly produce anti-Soviet governments.

The Russians thus may well have estimated the Western pressures as calculated to encourage their enemies in Eastern Europe and to defeat their own minimum objective of a protective glacis. Everything still hung, however, on the course of military operations. The wartime collaboration had been created by one thing, and one thing alone: the threat of Nazi victory. So long as this threat was real, so was the collaboration. In late December 1944, von Rundstedt launched his counteroffensive in the Ardennes. A few weeks later, when Roosevelt, Churchill, and Stalin gathered in the Crimea, it was in the shadow of this last considerable explosion of German power. The meeting at Yalta was still dominated by the mood of war.

Yalta remains something of an historical perplexity—less, from the perspective of 1967, because of a mythical American deference to the sphere-of-influence thesis than because of the documentable Russian deference to the universalist thesis. Why should Stalin in 1945 have accepted the Declaration on Liberated Europe and an agreement on Poland pledging that "the three governments will jointly" act to assure "free elections of governments responsive to the will of the people?" There are several probable answers: that the war was not over and the Russians still wanted the Americans to intensify their military effort in the West; that one clause in the Declaration premised action on "the opinion of the three governments" and thus implied a Soviet veto, though the Polish agreement was more definite; most of all that the universalist algebra of the Declaration was plainly in Stalin's mind to be construed in terms of the practical arithmetic of his sphere-of-influence agreement with Churchill the previous October. Stalin's assurance to Churchill at Yalta that a proposed Russian amendment to the Declaration would not apply to Greece makes it clear that Roosevelt's pieties did not, in Stalin's mind, nullify Churchill's percentages. He could well have been strengthened in this supposition by the fact that *after* Yalta, Churchill himself repeatedly reasserted the terms of the October agreement as if he regarded it, despite Yalta, as controlling.

Harriman still had the feeling before Yalta that the Kremlin had "two approaches to their postwar policies" and that Stalin himself was "of two minds." One approach emphasized the internal reconstruction and development of Russia; the other its external expansion. But in the meantime the fact which dominated all political decisions—that is, the war against Germany —was moving into its final phase. In the weeks after Yalta, the military situation changed with great rapidity. As the Nazi threat declined, so too did the need for cooperation. The Soviet Union, feeling itself menaced by the American idea of self-determination and the borderlands diplomacy to which it was leading, skeptical whether the United Nations would protect its frontiers as reliably as its own domination in Eastern Europe, began to fulfill its security requirements unilaterally.

In March Stalin expressed his evaluation of the United Nations by rejecting Roosevelt's plea that Molotov come to the San Francisco Conference, if only for the opening sessions. In the next weeks the Russians emphatically and crudely worked their will in Eastern Europe, above all in the test country of Poland. They were ignoring the Declaration on Liberated Europe, ignoring the Atlantic Charter, self-determination, human freedom, and everything else the Americans considered essential for a stable peace. "We must clearly recognize," Harriman wired Washington a few days before Roosevelt's death, "that the Soviet program is the establishment of totalitarianism, ending personal liberty and democracy as we know and respect it."

At the same time, the Russians also began to mobilize Communist resources in the United States itself to block American universalism. In April 1945 Jacques Duclos, who had been the

Comintern official responsible for the Western communist parties, launched in *Cahiers du Communisme* an uncompromising attack on the policy of the American Communist Party. Duclos sharply condemned the revisionism of Earl Browder, the American Communist leader, as "expressed in the concept of a long-term class peace in the United States, of the possibility of the suppression of the class struggle in the postwar period and of establishment of harmony between labor and capital." Browder was specifically rebuked for favoring the "self-determination" of Europe "west of the Soviet Union" on a bourgeois-democratic basis. The excommunication of Browderism was plainly the Politburo's considered reaction to the impending defeat of Germany; it was a signal to the Communist parties of the West that they should recover their identity; it was Moscow's alert to Communists everywhere that they should prepare for new policies in the postwar world.

The Duclos piece obviously could not have been planned and written much later than the Yalta conference—that is, well before a number of events which revisionists now cite in order to demonstrate American responsibility for the Cold War: before Allen Dulles, for example, began to negotiate the surrender of the German armies in Italy (the episode which provoked Stalin to charge Roosevelt with seeking a separate peace and provoked Roosevelt to denounce the "vile misrepresentations" of Stalin's informants); well before Roosevelt died; many months before the testing of the atomic bomb; even more months before Truman ordered that the bomb be dropped on Japan. William Z. Foster, who soon replaced Browder as the leader of the American Communist Party and embodied the new Moscow line, later boasted of having said in January 1944, "A postwar Roosevelt administration would continue to be, as it is now, an imperialist government." With ancient suspicions revived by the American insistence on universalism, this was no doubt the conclusion which the Russians were reaching at the same time. The Soviet canonization of Roosevelt (like their present-day canonization of Kennedy) took place after the American President's death.

The atmosphere of mutual suspicion was beginning to rise. In January 1945 Molotov formally proposed that the United States grant Russia a $6 billion credit for postwar reconstruction. With characteristic tact he explained that he was doing this as a favor to save America from a postwar depression. The proposal seems to have been diffidently made and diffidently received. Roosevelt requested that the matter "not be pressed further" on the American side until he had a chance to talk with Stalin; but the Russians did not follow it up either at Yalta in February (save for a single glancing reference) or during the Stalin-Hopkins talks in May or at Potsdam. Finally the proposal was renewed in the very different political atmosphere of August. This time Washington inexplicably mislaid the request during the transfer of the records of the Foreign Economic Administration to the State Department. It did not turn up again until March 1946. Of course this was impossible for the Russians to believe; it is hard enough even for those acquainted with the capacity of the American government for incompetence to believe; and it only strengthened Soviet suspicions of American purposes.

The American credit was one conceivable form of Western contribution to Russian reconstruction. Another was lend-lease, and the possibility of reconstruction aid under the lend-lease protocol had already been discussed in 1944. But in May 1945 Russia, like Britain, suffered from Truman's abrupt termination of lend-lease shipments—"unfortunate and even brutal," Stalin told Hopkins, adding that, if it was "designed as pressure on the Russians in order to soften them up, then it was a fundamental mistake." A third form was German reparations. Here Stalin in demanding $10 billion in reparations for the Soviet Union made his strongest fight at Yalta. Roosevelt, while agreeing essentially with Churchill's opposition, tried to postpone the matter by accepting the Soviet figure as a "basis for discussion"— a formula which led to future misunderstanding. In short, the Russian hope for major Western assistance in postwar reconstruction foundered on three events which the Kremlin could well have interpreted respectively as deliberate sabotage (the loan request), blackmail (lend-lease cancellation), and pro-Germanism (reparations).

Actually the American attempt to settle the fourth lend-lease protocol was generous and the Russians for their own reasons declined to come to an agreement. It is not clear, though, that satisfying Moscow on any of these financial scores would have made much essential difference. It might have persuaded some doves in the Kremlin that the U.S. government was genuinely friendly; it might have persuaded some hawks that the American anxiety for Soviet friendship was such that Moscow could do as it wished without inviting challenge from the United States. It would, in short, merely have reinforced both sides of the Kremlin debate; it would hardly have reversed deeper tendencies toward the deterioration of political relationships. Economic deals were surely subordinate to the quality of mutual political confidence; and here, in the months after Yalta, the decay was steady.

The Cold War had now begun. It was the product not of a decision but of a dilemma. Each side felt compelled to adopt policies which the other could not but regard as a threat to the principles of the peace. Each then felt compelled to undertake defensive measures. Thus the Russians saw no choice but to consolidate their security in Eastern Europe. The Americans, regarding Eastern Europe as the first step toward Western Europe, responded by asserting their interest in the zone the Russians deemed vital to their security. The Russians concluded that the West was resuming its old course of capitalist encirclement; that it was purposefully laying the foundation for anti-Soviet regimes in the area defined by the blood of centuries as crucial to Russian survival. Each side believed with passion that future international stability depended on the success of its own conception of world order. Each side, in pursuing its own clearly indicated and deeply cherished principles, was only confirming the fear of the other that it was bent on aggression.

Very soon the process began to acquire a cumulative momentum. The impending collapse of Germany thus provoked new troubles: the Russians, for example, sincerely feared that the West was planning a separate surrender of the German armies in Italy in a way which would release troops for Hitler's eastern front, as they subsequently feared that the Nazis might succeed in surrendering Berlin to the West. This was the context in which the atomic bomb now appeared. Though the revisionist argument that Truman dropped the bomb less to defeat Japan than to intimidate Russia is not convincing, this thought unquestionably appealed to some in Washington as at least an advantageous side effect of Hiroshima.

So the machinery of suspicion and counter suspicion, action, and counter action, was set in motion. But, given relations among traditional national states, there was still no reason, even with all the postwar jostling, why this should not have remained a manageable situation. What made it unmanageable, what caused the rapid escalation of the Cold War and in another two years completed the division of Europe, was a set of considerations which this account has thus far excluded.

Up to this point, the discussion has considered the schism within the wartime coalition as if it were entirely the result of disagreements among national states. Assuming this framework, there was unquestionably a failure of communication between America and Russia, a misperception of signals and, as time went on, a mounting tendency to ascribe ominous motives to the other side. It seems hard, for example, to deny that American postwar policy created genuine difficulties for the Russians and even assumed a threatening aspect for them. All this the revisionists have rightly and usefully emphasized.

But the great omission of the revisionists—and also the fundamental explanation of the speed with which the Cold War escalated—lies precisely in the fact that the Soviet Union was *not* a traditional national state.[4] This is where the "mirror image,"

---

[4] This is the classical revisionist fallacy—the assumption of the rationality, or at least of the traditionalism, of states where ideology and social organization have created a different range of motives. So the Second World War revisionists omit the totalitarian dynamism of Nazism and the fanati-

invoked by some psychologists, falls down. For the Soviet Union was a phenomenon very different from America or Britain: it was a totalitarian state, endowed with an all-explanatory, all-consuming ideology, committed to the infallibility of government and party, still in a somewhat messianic mood, equating dissent with treason, and ruled by a dictator who, for all his quite extraordinary abilities, had his paranoid moments.

Marxism-Leninism gave the Russian leaders a view of the world according to which all societies were inexorably destined to proceed along appointed roads by appointed stages until they achieved the classless nirvana. Moreover, given the resistance of the capitalists to this development, the existence of any non-communist state was *by definition* a threat to the Soviet Union. "As long as capitalism and socialism exist," Lenin wrote, "we cannot live in peace: in the end, one or the other will triumph—a funeral dirge will be sung either over the Soviet Republic or over world capitalism."

Stalin and his associates, whatever Roosevelt or Truman did or failed to do, were bound to regard the United States as the enemy not because of this deed or that, but because of the primordial fact that America was the leading capitalist power and thus, by Leninist syllogism, unappeasably hostile, driven by the logic of its system to oppose, encircle, and destroy Soviet Russia. Nothing the United States could have done in 1944–1945 would have abolished this mistrust, required and sanctified as it was by Marxist gospel—nothing short of the conversion of the United States into a Stalinist despotism; and even this would not have sufficed, as the experience of Jugoslavia and China soon showed, unless it were accompanied by total subservience to Moscow. So long as the United States remained a capitalist democracy, no American policy, given Moscow's theology, could hope to win basic Soviet confidence, and every American action

---

cism of Hitler, as the Civil War revisionists omit the fact that the slavery system was producing a doctrinaire closed society in the American South. For a consideration of some of these issues, see "The Causes of the Civil War: A Note on Historical Sentimentalism" in my *The Politics of Hope* (Boston: Houghton Mifflin, 1963).

was poisoned from the source. So long as the Soviet Union remained a messianic state, ideology compelled a steady expansion of Communist power.

It is easy, of course, to exaggerate the capacity of ideology to control events. The tension of acting according to revolutionary abstractions is too much for most nations to sustain over a long period: that is why Mao Tse-tung has launched his Cultural Revolution, hoping thereby to create a permanent revolutionary mood and save Chinese communism from the degeneration which, in his view, has overtaken Russian communism. Still, as any revolution grows older, normal human and social motives will increasingly reassert themselves. In due course, we can be sure, Leninism will be about as effective in governing the daily lives of Russians as Christianity is in governing the daily lives of Americans. Like the Ten Commandments and the Sermon on the Mount, the Leninist verities will increasingly become platitudes for ritual observance, not guides to secular decision. There can be no worse fallacy (even if respectable people practiced it diligently for a season in the United States) than that of drawing from a nation's ideology permanent conclusions about its behavior.

A temporary recession of ideology was already taking place during the Second World War when Stalin, to rally his people against the invader, had to replace the appeal of Marxism by that of nationalism. ("We are under no illusions that they are fighting for us," Stalin once said to Harriman. "They are fighting for Mother Russia.") But this was still taking place within the strictest limitations. The Soviet Union remained as much a police state as ever; the regime was as infallible as ever; foreigners and their ideas were as suspect as ever. "Never, except possibly during my later experience as ambassador in Moscow," Kennan has written, "did the insistence of the Soviet authorities on isolation of the diplomatic corps weigh more heavily on me . . . than in these first weeks following my return to Russia in the final months of the war. . . . [We were] treated as though we were the bearers of some species of the plague"—which, of course, from the Soviet viewpoint, they were: the plague of skepticism.

Paradoxically, of the forces capable of bringing about a modification of ideology, the most practical and effective was the Soviet dictatorship itself. If Stalin was an ideologist, he was also a pragmatist. If he saw everything through the lenses of Marxism-Leninism, he also, as the infallible expositor of the faith, could reinterpret Marxism-Leninism to justify anything he wanted to do at any given moment. No doubt Roosevelt's ignorance of Marxism-Leninism was inexcusable and led to grievous miscalculations. But Roosevelt's efforts to work on and through Stalin were not so hopelessly naive as it used to be fashionable to think. With the extraordinary instinct of a great political leader, Roosevelt intuitively understood that Stalin was the *only* lever available to the West against the Leninist ideology and the Soviet system. If Stalin could be reached, then alone was there a chance of getting the Russians to act contrary to the prescriptions of their faith. The best evidence is that Roosevelt retained a certain capacity to influence Stalin to the end; the nominal Soviet acquiescence in American universalism as late as Yalta was perhaps an indication of that. It is in this way that the death of Roosevelt was crucial—not in the vulgar sense that his policy was then reversed by his successor, which did not happen, but in the sense that no other American could hope to have the restraining impact on Stalin which Roosevelt might for a while have had.

Stalin alone could have made any difference. Yet Stalin, in spite of the impression of sobriety and realism he made on Westerners who saw him during the Second World War, was plainly a man of deep and morbid obsessions and compulsions. When he was still a young man, Lenin had criticized his rude and arbitrary ways. A reasonably authoritative observer (N. S. Khrushchev) later commented, "These negative characteristics of his developed steadily and during the last years acquired an absolutely insufferable character." His paranoia, probably set off by the suicide of his wife in 1932, led to the terrible purges of the mid-thirties and the wanton murder of thousands of his Bolshevik comrades. "Everywhere and in everything," Khrushchev says of this period, "he saw 'enemies,' 'double-dealers,' and 'spies.' "

The crisis of war evidently steadied him in some way, though Khrushchev speaks of his "nervousness and hysteria . . . even after the war began." The madness, so rigidly controlled for a time, burst out with new and shocking intensity in the postwar years. "After the war," Khrushchev testifies,

> the situation became even more complicated. Stalin became even more capricious, irritable and brutal; in particular, his suspicion grew. His persecution mania reached unbelievable dimensions. . . . He decided everything, without any consideration for anyone or anything.
>
> Stalin's wilfulness showed itself . . . also in the international relations of the Soviet Union. . . . He had completely lost a sense of reality; he demonstrated his suspicion and haughtiness not only in relation to individuals in the USSR, but in relation to whole parties and nations.

A revisionist fallacy has been to treat Stalin as just another Realpolitik statesman, as Second World War revisionists see Hitler as just another Stresemann or Bismarck. But the record makes it clear that in the end nothing could satisfy Stalin's paranoia. His own associates failed. Why does anyone suppose that any conceivable American policy would have succeeded?

An analysis of the origins of the Cold War which leaves out these factors—the intransigence of Leninist ideology, the sinister dynamics of a totalitarian society and the madness of Stalin—is obviously incomplete. It was these factors which made it hard for the West to accept the thesis that Russia was moved only by a desire to protect its security and would be satisfied by the control of Eastern Europe; it was these factors which charged the debate between universalism and spheres of influence with apocalyptic potentiality.

Leninism and totalitarianism created a structure of thought and behavior which made postwar collaboration between Russia and America—in any normal sense of civilized intercourse between national states—inherently impossible. The Soviet dictatorship of 1945 simply could not have survived such a collaboration. Indeed, nearly a quarter-century later, the Soviet regime, though it has meanwhile moved a good distance, could still hardly survive it without risking the release inside Russia of energies profoundly opposed to Communist despotism. As for Stalin, he may have represented the only force in 1945 capable of overcoming Stalinism, but the very traits which enabled him to win absolute power expressed terrifying instabilities of mind and temperament and hardly offered a solid foundation for a peaceful world.

The difference between America and Russia in 1945 was that some Americans fundamentally believed that, over a long run, a *modus vivendi* with Russia was possible; while the Russians, so far as one can tell, believed in no more than a short-run *modus vivendi* with the United States.

Harriman and Kennan, this narrative has made clear, took the lead in warning Washington about the difficulties of short-run dealings with the Soviet Union. But both argued that, if the United States developed a rational policy and stuck to it, there would be, after long and rough passages, the prospect of eventual clearing. "I am, as you know," Harriman cabled Washington in early April, "a most earnest advocate of the closest possible understanding with the Soviet Union so that what I am saying relates only to how best to attain such understanding." Kennan has similarly made it clear that the function of his containment policy was "to tide us over a difficult time and bring us to the point where we could discuss effectively with the Russians the dangers and drawbacks this *status quo* involved, and to arrange with them for its peaceful replacement by a better and sounder one." The subsequent careers of both men attest to the honesty of these statements.

There is no corresponding evidence on the Russian side that anyone seriously sought a *modus vivendi* in these terms. Stalin's choice was whether his long-term ideological and national interests would be better served by a short-run truce with the West or by an immediate resumption of pressure. In October 1945 Stalin indicated to Harriman at Sochi that he planned to adopt the second course—that the Soviet Union was going isolationist.

No doubt the succession of problems with the United States contributed to this decision, but the basic causes most probably lay elsewhere: in the developing situations in Eastern Europe, in Western Europe, and in the United States.

In Eastern Europe, Stalin was still for a moment experimenting with techniques of control. But he must by now have begun to conclude that he had underestimated the hostility of the people to Russian dominion. The Hungarian elections in November would finally convince him that the Yalta formula was a road to anti-Soviet governments. At the same time, he was feeling more strongly than ever a sense of his opportunities in Western Europe. The other half of the Continent lay unexpectedly before him, politically demoralized, economically prostrate, militarily defenseless. The hunting would be better and safer than he had anticipated. As for the United States, the alacrity of postwar demobilization must have recalled Roosevelt's offhand remark at Yalta that "two years would be the limit" for keeping American troops in Europe. And, despite Dr. Eugene Varga's doubts about the imminence of American economic breakdown, Marxist theology assured Stalin that the United States was heading into a bitter postwar depression and would be consumed with its own problems. If the condition of Eastern Europe made unilateral action seem essential in the interests of Russian security, the condition of Western Europe and the United States offered new temptations for Communist expansion. The Cold War was now in full swing.

It still had its year of modulations and accommodations. Secretary Byrnes conducted his long and fruitless campaign to persuade the Russians that America only sought governments in Eastern Europe "both friendly to the Soviet Union and representative of all the democratic elements of the country." Crises were surmounted in Trieste and Iran. Secretary Marshall evidently did not give up hope of a *modus vivendi* until the Moscow conference of foreign secretaries of March 1947. Even then, the Soviet Union was invited to participate in the Marshall Plan.

The point of no return came on July 2, 1947, when Molotov, after bringing 89 technical specialists with him to Paris and evincing initial interest in the project for European reconstruction, received the hot flash from the Kremlin, denounced the whole idea and walked out of the conference. For the next fifteen years the Cold War raged unabated, passing out of historical ambiguity into the realm of good versus evil and breeding on both sides simplifications, stereotypes, and self-serving absolutes, often couched in interchangeable phrases. Under the pressure even America, for a deplorable decade, forsook its pragmatic and pluralist traditions, posed as God's appointed messenger to ignorant and sinful man and followed the Soviet example in looking to a world remade in its own image.

In retrospect, if it is impossible to see the Cold War as a case of American aggression and Russian response, it is also hard to see it as a pure case of Russian aggression and American response. "In what is truly tragic," wrote Hegel, "there must be valid moral powers on both the sides which come into collision. . . . Both suffer loss and yet both are mutually justified." In this sense, the Cold War had its tragic elements. The question remains whether it was an instance of Greek tragedy—as Auden has called it, "the tragedy of necessity," where the feeling aroused in the spectator is "What a pity it had to be this way"—or of Christian tragedy, "the tragedy of possibility," where the feeling aroused is "What a pity it was this way when it might have been otherwise."

Once something has happened, the historian is tempted to assume that it had to happen; but this may often be a highly unphilosophical assumption. The Cold War could have been avoided only if the Soviet Union had not been possessed by convictions both of the infallibility of the Communist word and of the inevitability of a Communist world. These convictions transformed an impasse between national states into a religious war, a tragedy of possibility into one of necessity. One might wish that America had preserved the poise and proportion of the first years of the Cold War and had not in time succumbed to its own forms of self-righteousness. But the most rational of American policies could hardly have averted the Cold War. Only today, as Russia begins to recede from its messianic mission and to accept, in practice if not yet in principle, the permanence of the world of diversity, only now can the hope flicker that this long, dreary, costly contest may at last be taking on forms less dramatic, less obsessive and less dangerous to the future of mankind.

# 3

# Hans J. Morgenthau

*Born in Germany in 1904, and educated at European universities, Hans J. Morgenthau is recognized as one of America's foremost students of international relations. Among his published works are* Politics Among Nations *(New York: Knopf, 1948),* The Purpose of American Politics *(New York: Knopf, 1960),* Politics in the Twentieth Century *(Chicago: University of Chicago Press, 1962), and* A New Foreign Policy for the United States *(New York: Praeger, 1969). Mr. Morgenthau is Leonard Davis Distinguished Professor in Political Science at The City University of New York, and Albert A. Michelson Distinguished Service Professor of Political Science and Modern History at The University of Chicago.*

*The present essay was written by Mr. Morgenthau especially for The American Forum Series.*

Two factors distinguish the Cold War between the Soviet Union and the West from the many hostile confrontations history records and, hence, justify its name. The first factor was the impossibility for all concerned, given the interests at stake and the positions taken, to pursue conciliatory policies through compromise, which might have led to a settlement of the outstanding issues. The second was the necessity, following from this impossibility, for both sides to protect and promote their interests through unilateral direct pressure on the opponent's will by all means available—diplomatic, military, economic, subversive—short of the actual use of force. Thus we have been in a "war" because the purpose was not to accommodate the other side in return for reciprocal accommodations, but rather to compel the other side to yield. "Rollback" and "liberation" are terms of war which imply not a mutual accommodation but a unilateral action. The threat of military force, if the other side should not yield its position in West Berlin, has the same characteristic.

But while both sides have used the techniques of war rather than diplomacy to achieve their ends, they have been very careful not to resort to force, at least in their relations with each other. Thus we have been in a "war" insofar as unilateral techniques are the instruments of war and not of diplomacy; and the war has been a "cold" one because the use of force upon a major opponent was excluded from the instruments of unilateral action. In Raymond Aron's trenchant formulation, peace is impossible while war is improbable.

## The Origins

Applying Aron's analysis to the relations between the Soviet Union and the West, which have gone by the name of Cold War since the end of World War II, one is able to determine at least the general period of history during which this particular Cold War began. It started when the statesmen became aware of the impossibility of peace and the improbability of war and when this deadlock began to dominate the foreign policies pursued. This process started at Yalta in 1944 and was consummated with the establishment of the North Atlantic Treaty Organization in 1949. To fix a different period of history for the beginning of the Cold War, for example, the middle of the nineteenth century, or 1917, as some historians have done,[1] requires a different definition of Cold War, which would deprive the concept of its unique meaning. For the conflict between Russia and the West, which dominated the political world of the nineteenth

---

[1] Cf. Desmond Donnelly, *Struggle for the World. The Cold War: 1917–1965* (New York: St. Martin's Press, 1965) and André Fontaine, *History of the Cold War from the October Revolution to the Korean War, 1917–1950* (New York: Pantheon Books, 1968).

century, did not render peace impossible nor war improbable. It led to the Crimean War in 1853, as well as to the settlement of Berlin in 1878. On the other hand, the ascendancy of bolshevism as a world revolutionary movement in 1917, made peace indeed impossible but by no means made war improbable—as shown by the allied intervention in 1918–1919, the war between the Soviet Union and Poland in 1921, the war between the Soviet Union and Finland in 1939–1940, and World War II.

The Cold War between the Soviet Union and the West owes its existence to the unique coincidence of two historic factors in the aftermath of World War II: First, the impossibility of peace because of conflicting, incompatible conceptions of the postwar world, which rendered both sides more intractable by dint of their identification with incompatible, ideological positions and aspirations; and second, the improbability of war because of the possibility of nuclear war.

## The Possibility of Nuclear War

In the prenuclear age these conflicts between incompatible political conceptions and ideologies, in all likelihood, would have been resolved by war. A statesman of the prenuclear age could and did ask himself whether he could achieve his goals by the peaceful means of diplomacy or whether he had to resort to force with the threat or the actuality of war. His calculations might turn out to be faulty or be brought to nought by accident, but they were in themselves perfectly rational.

These calculations have remained rational insofar as they apply to conventional force in a nonnuclear context. Thus, India and Pakistan and Israel and the Arab states acted rationally when they continued to use conventional force as an instrument of their national policies. One can even make a case for the rationality of the use of conventional force in a nuclear context, provided adequate precautions are taken to insulate the use of conventional force from the nuclear context. The Korean War is a case in point.

However, this rational relationship that has existed from the beginning of history to 1945 between force as a means and the ends of foreign policy does not apply to nuclear weapons. The destructiveness of nuclear weapons is so enormous that it overwhelms all possible objectives of a rational foreign policy. Nuclear weapons, if they were used as instruments of national policy, would destroy the tangible objective of the policy and the belligerents as well. In consequence, these weapons are not susceptible to rational use as instruments of national policy. Thus, nuclear war has become improbable.

## The Responsibility

At the same time, peace remained impossible for political and ideological reasons. The causes of this stalemate have recently became the subject of scholarly controversy in the United States. The official and widely held popular version attributes all responsibility for the Cold War to the policies Stalin pursued during the last year of and during the aftermath of World War II. More particularly, the origin of the Cold War is traced to the Soviet violations of the Yalta agreements. At this point, the official and popular version divides into two schools of thought. Some see in Stalin a mere exponent of the unalterable attitudes and objectives of communism; and others concentrate all the blame on Stalin as a person in contrast to Khrushchev and his successors who are credited with the desire to "make an end to the Cold War." The accounts of C. B. Marshall[2] and Paul Seabury[3] lean towards the former view, while Marshall Shulman's book,[4] primarily policy-oriented, points in the other direction.

Against this view, which has been both a result and an instrument of the Cold War, a twofold reaction has set in. One is revisionist and polemical, a kind of counterfoil to the view it opposes in trying to show how much the United States was

---

[2] Charles Burton Marshall, *The Cold War: A Concise History* (New York: Franklin Watts, 1965).

[3] Paul Seabury, *The Rise and Decline of the Cold War* (New York: Basic Books, 1967).

[4] Marshall D. Shulman, *Beyond the Cold War* (New Haven: Yale University Press, 1966).

to blame for the Cold War. D. F. Fleming's massive attack upon the official doctrine[5] is in good measure a Cold-War polemic in reverse, shifting the principal blame from the Soviet Union to the United States. Gar Alperovitz[6] set himself the more limited task of showing that the atomic bomb was used against Japan not primarily for military reasons but as a political weapon in the confrontation with the Soviet Union.

The other reaction transcends the polemics of the Cold War. It lets the diplomatic record speak for itself, as does Martin Herz,[7] or it assesses the merits and demerits of each side's case with an impressive measure of philosophic detachment, as do Walter LaFeber,[8] John Lukacs,[9] and Louis Halle.[10] The record is made particularly eloquent in Mr. Herz's book through the seventy-eight questions and answers summarizing the conclusions to be drawn from the analysis. Or this reaction seeks to substitute for the enmities and rivalries of traditional power politics an altogether new type of foreign policy aiming at a world community, as does the Barnet-Raskin volume.[11]

The picture of the origins of the Cold War that emerges from these books was already foreshadowed by Walter Lippmann's analysis[12] and by other earlier accounts, based upon primary sources, by Herbert Feis[13] and William H. McNeill.[14] It is

---

[5] D. F. Fleming, *The Cold War and Its Origins* (London: Allen & Unwin, 1961).

[6] Gar Alperovitz, *Atomic Diplomacy: Hiroshima and Potsdam* (New York: Simon & Schuster, 1965).

[7] Martin F. Herz, *Beginnings of the Cold War* (Bloomington: Indiana University Press, 1966).

[8] Walter LaFeber, *America, Russia, and the Cold War, 1945–1966* (New York: John Wiley and Sons, 1967).

[9] John Lukacs, *A New History of the Cold War* (New York: Doubleday, 1966).

[10] Louis J. Halle, *The Cold War as History* (London: Chatto & Windus, 1967).

[11] Richard J. Barnet and Marcus S. Raskin, *After 20 Years: Alternatives to the Cold War in Europe* (New York: Random House, 1965).

[12] Walter Lippmann, *The Cold War* (New York, Harper and Brothers, 1947).

[13] Herbert Feis, *Churchill, Roosevelt, Stalin: The War They Waged and the Peace They Sought* (Princeton: Princeton University Press, 1957).

[14] William H. McNeill, *America, Britain and Russia: Their Co-operation and Conflict, 1941–1946* (New York: Oxford University Press, 1953).

starkly at variance with the official and popular view. It is centered upon two divergent and incompatible conceptions of the postwar world: The first visualizes one world united in an effective universal organization; the other sees the world organized into strictly defined spheres of influence dominated by the great powers.

## Spheres of Influence Versus Universalism

Since World War II, the Soviet Union has been the foremost practitioner of a spheres-of-influence policy, while the United States has been opposed to spheres of influence as a matter of principle. The Soviet Union never hid its desire to acquire a sphere of influence in Eastern Europe and to divide the rest of the world into such spheres as well. According to the "Secret Additional Protocol" to the Treaty of Non-Aggression of August 23, 1939, better known as the Molotov-Ribbentrop Pact, the Soviet Union and Germany "discussed in strictly confidential conversations the question of the boundaries of their respective spheres of influence." During World War II, the Soviet Union persistently pressed Great Britain for a spheres-of-influence agreement dividing Europe, and while Great Britain appeared agreeable, the United States was as persistently opposed. It was in the face of that temporarily relenting opposition that Churchill and Stalin, on October 9th, 1944, concluded personally and most informally an agreement dividing the Balkans into Soviet and non-Soviet spheres of influence. The agreement gave the Soviet Union 90 per cent dominance in Rumania and 75 per cent in Bulgaria, divided Soviet and Western influence equally in Hungary and Yugoslavia, and allotted Great Britain 90 per cent predominance in Greece. After the war, the Soviet Union made numerous proposals for the division of the world into two gigantic spheres of influence, dominated respectively by the Soviet Union and the United States. While these proposals were never officially acknowledged by the United States, they were occasionally referred to in the press. In the *New York Times* of March 13, 1950, for instance, James Reston reported such a proposal under the heading "Soviet Move Seen for Deal with U.S. to Divide World" and concluded that "there is no evidence that officials here are even slightly interested in such a deal."

This lack of interest was not limited to the officials of the day; rather it reflects a consistent opposition to spheres of influence of any kind. During World War II, Secretary of State Cordell Hull was in the forefront of that opposition. In his *Memoirs*, he declared not to be "a believer in the idea of balance of power or spheres of influence as a means of keeping the peace." When he reported to Congress on November 18, 1943 on the Moscow Conference which had agreed on the establishment of the United Nations, he declared that "there will no longer be need for spheres of influence, for alliances, for balance of power, or any other of the special arrangements through which, in the unhappy past, the nations strove to safeguard their security or promote their interests." And Franklin D. Roosevelt stated as a matter of fact on March 1, 1945 in his report to Congress on the Yalta Conference: "The Crimean Conference . . . spells the end of the system of unilateral action and exclusive alliances and spheres of influence and balances of power and all the other expedients which have been tried for centuries—and have failed."

This opposition to spheres of influence is rooted in two tenets of American political philosophy: The availability of a viable alternative to "power politics" in the form of a universal, international organization and the universal applicability of democratic procedures and institutions as a remedy for political ills. The first tenet is clearly and consistently expressed in Hull's utterances. Recalling in his *Memoirs* his opposition to a Soviet sphere of influence in Eastern Europe, he wrote:

> I could sympathize fully with Stalin's desire to protect his Western borders from future attack. But I felt that this security could best be obtained through a strong postwar peace organization. . . . It seemed to me that any creation of zones of influence would inevitably sow the seeds of future conflict. I felt that zones of influence could not but derogate from the overall authority of the international security organizations which I expected would come into being.

In other words, nations have a choice between traditional "power politics" with all its moral liabilities and political risks, of which spheres of influence form an intrinsic part, and a new and different kind of foreign policy, free of these liabilities and risks.

The other tenet has been most eloquently formulated by Woodrow Wilson in his message to the Senate on January 22, 1917:

> No peace can last, or ought to last, which does not recognize and accept the principle that governments derive all their just powers from the consent of the governed and that no right anywhere exists to hand peoples about from potentate to potentate as if they were property. . . . I am proposing, as it were, that the nations should with one accord adopt the doctrine of President Monroe as the doctrine of the world: that no nation should seek to extend its polity over any other nation or people, but that every people should be left free to determine its own polity, its own way of development, unhindered, unthreatened, unafraid, the little along with the great and powerful.

At Yalta and at the conferences and diplomatic exchanges following it our insistence upon democratic governments for the nations of Eastern Europe became the main ideological weapon with which we tried to nullify the transformation of Eastern Europe into a Soviet sphere of influence.

However, this opposition to spheres of influence as a matter of principle has been completely at odds not only with the Soviet conception of international order but also with two facets of our own foreign policy: The championship of a sphere of influence when it was supposed to serve our interests, and our acquiescence, as a matter of fact, in the Soviet sphere of influence in Eastern Europe.

The Monroe Doctrine, which stipulates the exclusion of European political institutions and territorial acquisitions from the Western Hemisphere and thereby allows the preponderance of the United States free play, is the most comprehensive, unilateral proclamation of a sphere of influence of modern times. American statesmen have not hesitated to refer to the Western Hemisphere or part of it as an American sphere of influence. Secretary of State Robert Lansing, invoking the Monroe Doctrine as well as more specific American interests, wrote in a state paper addressed to President Wilson that "The Caribbean is within the peculiar sphere of influence of the United States. . . ." It was none other than Woodrow Wilson who said that "In adopting the Monroe Doctrine the United States assumed the part of Big Brother to the rest of America," and who referred to the Western Hemisphere as an "implied and partial protectorate." The inconsistency of accepting the Western Hemisphere as an American sphere of influence and opposing, as a matter of principle, all other spheres of influence moved Winston Churchill, defending his deal with Stalin on the Balkans against the American opposition, to write to the British Ambassador in Washington:

> On the other hand, we follow the lead of the United States in South America as far as possible, as long as it is not a question of our beef and mutton. On this we naturally develop strong views on account of the little we get.

American opposition to spheres of influence per se is not only inconsistent with American practice in the Western Hemisphere, but it is also inconsistent with American practice in regard to that sphere of influence which provoked our most strenuous opposition—the Soviet sphere in Eastern Europe. The conflict between ourselves and the Soviet Union, which is at the root of the Cold War, arose at Yalta from incompatible conceptions and aspirations concerning the shape of the postwar world. The Soviet Union, following in the footsteps of Czarist Russia, wanted an exclusive sphere of influence in Eastern Europe. The West wanted to keep at least a measure of influence in that region through the instrumentality of democratic governments which, however, were supposed to be friendly to the Soviet Union.

Yet Stalin saw the inner contradiction of that proposal and did not hesitate to resolve it in favor of the Soviet Union. "A freely elected government in any of these countries", he observed at Yalta, "would be anti-Soviet, and that we cannot allow." The Red Army, already in control of Eastern Europe, guaranteed that what the Soviet Union could not allow would not come to pass. Thus what the United States sought to achieve at Yalta was impossible as long as the Red Army was in control in Eastern Europe. When President Roosevelt reported to Congress that "The Crimean Conference . . . spells the end of the system of unilateral action . . . spheres of influence . . . and all the other expedients which have been tried for centuries," he intended to proclaim victory for the American conception of the postwar world. In truth, he ratified, without knowing it, the triumph of the Soviet conception. For it was exactly through this "system of unilateral action . . . spheres of influence . . . and all the other expedients" of traditional power politics that Stalin intended to, and actually did, secure the interests of the Soviet Union. The briefing book that President Truman took with him to the Potsdam Conference in July 1945 summarized the situation in these laconic terms: "Eastern Europe is, in fact, a Soviet sphere of influence."

American rhetoric refused to reconcile itself to this fact. As the Soviet Union has reproached us for refusing to recognize its sphere of influence, so we have reproached the Soviet Union for having acquired it. More than that, for about a decade following the end of the war, we have intimated through slogans such as "Liberation" and "Rollback" that we were contemplating a policy to undo what Stalin had achieved. But, as the London *Economist* pointed out on August 30, 1952, "Unhappily 'liberation' applied to Eastern Europe—and Asia—means either the risk of war or it means nothing. . . . 'Liberation' entails no risk of war only when it means nothing."

Its intent became obvious when the United States remained inactive on the occasion of the German uprising of 1953, the Polish revolt and Hungarian Revolution of 1956, and the Soviet occupation of Czechoslovakia in 1968. The latter two events are particularly revealing since the President declared from the outset, in the case of the Hungarian Revolution, that he would refrain from intervening on behalf of democracy and against exclusive Soviet control. We are not concerned with the merits of this policy of abstention, but only with its bearing upon the American opposition to spheres of influence, especially to the Soviet sphere in Eastern Europe. Our policy of abstention, reducing "liberation" to nothing, by the same token amounted to the implicit recognition of the Soviet sphere of influence. What we had refused to do explicitly at Yalta and ever since, we have done implicitly through consistent inaction. Our inaction repudiated our policy at Yalta and our rhetoric following it, as well as the moral principles on which both were based.

Not only have American policies concerning spheres of influence been at odds in different periods of history, but the official opposition to spheres of influence has been challenged by the highest political authority, the President himself. One such challenge remained without practical results. It is reported in a memorandum by the late Cardinal Spellman entitled "Here are a few outstanding points of the conversation" the Cardinal had with President Roosevelt on September 3, 1943. Under the subheading "Collaboration of the 'Big Four' " we read:

> It is planned to make an agreement among the Big Four. Accordingly the world will be divided into spheres of influence: China gets the Far East; the U.S. the Pacific; Britain and Russia, Europe and Africa. But as Britain has predominantly colonial interests it might be assumed that Russia will predominate in Europe. Although Chiang Kai-shek will be called in on the great decisions concerning Europe, it is understood that he will have no influence on them. The same thing might become true—although to a lesser degree—for the U.S. He hoped, although it might be wishful thinking, that the Russian intervention in Europe would not be too harsh.

The other challenge, operating within President Roosevelt's mind as well as between himself, on the one hand, and Cordell Hull and Harry Hopkins, on the other, concerns the British-Soviet spheres-of-influence agreement with regard to the Balkans.

Churchill informed Roosevelt of his plan, and Roosevelt ordered an approving cable sent to Churchill. Hopkins intercepted the cable and persuaded Roosevelt to send instead a cable to Stalin, reaffirming the American opposition to spheres of influence.

> There is in this global war literally no question, either military or political . . . in which the United States is not interested. You will naturally understand this. It is my firm conviction that the solution to still unsolved questions can be found only by the three of us together. Therefore, while I appreciate the necessity for the present meeting, I choose to consider your forthcoming talks with Mr. Churchill merely as preliminary to a conference of the three of us. . . .

However, Roosevelt approved the deal once it was made, while Hull remained strenuously opposed.

Spheres of influence, as Churchill and Stalin knew and as Roosevelt recognized sporadically, have not been created by evil and benighted statesmen and, hence, cannot be abolished by an act of will on the part of good and enlightened ones. Like the balance of power, alliances, arms races, political and military rivalries and conflicts, and the rest of "power politics"—spheres of influence are the ineluctable byproduct of the interplay of interests and power in a society of sovereign nations. If you want to rid the world of spheres of influence and the other expedients of power politics, you must transform that society of sovereign nations into a supranational one, whose sovereign government can set effective limits to the expansionism of the nations composing it. Spheres of influence are one of the symptoms of the "disease," if this is what you want to call power politics, and it is at best futile and at worst mischievous to try to extirpate the symptom while leaving the cause unattended.

Thus the American political mind is engaged in a three-cornered war. It is at war with the political realities, which do not yield to the invocation of moral principles. It is at war with its moral principles, since it must condone implicitly what it condemns explicitly and is powerless to change. And it is at war again with its moral principles, since it practices with a good conscience what it condemns in others. It bridges the gap between its moral principles and its political practices by juxtaposing its selfless intentions with the evil purposes of other nations—most eloquently propounded, for instance, by Wilson in justification of the intervention in Mexico.

The war with the political realities has proven to be a quixotic futility, creating hopes sure to be disappointed and inciting actions doomed to fail. One war with moral principles opens up a gap between words and deeds, suggesting political weakness. The other war with moral principles issues in a self-confident pragmatism, which, in the best British tradition, combines moral assurance with political advantage.

A classic example of this combination is provided by the telephone conversation which was held between Secretary of War Henry Stimson and Assistant Secretary of War John McCloy in May 1945. The issue was how to combine the exclusiveness of the American sphere of influence in the Western Hemisphere with the international organization then planned. Both officials agreed that the formation of similar spheres in Europe and Asia for the benefit of the Soviet Union would conjure up the risk of war and destroy the effectiveness of the international organization. They also agreed that the exclusive American sphere in the Americas, where the United States could act unilaterally, must be preserved: "I think," said Stimson, "that it's not asking too much to have our little region over here which never has bothered anybody." They further agreed that the Soviet Union could not object to such an arrangement since it was building a similar sphere in Eastern Europe. Finally, they agreed that, according to McCloy, "we have a very strong interest in being able to intervene promptly in Europe . . . we ought to have our cake and eat it too; that we ought to be free to operate under this regional arrangement in South America, at the same time intervene promptly in Europe; that we oughtn't to give away either asset." Both denied that the position the United States occupied in the Western Hemisphere was analogous to the one the Soviet Union aspired to in Europe because our intervention in the Western Hemisphere did not upset the world balance of power while Soviet intervention in Europe would.

## Communism Versus the Free World

This conflict between two incompatible conceptions of the postwar world, by itself, was nothing more than a repetition of the conflict that pitted Wilsonianism against the power politics of Lloyd George and Clemenceau at the end of World War I. If there had been nothing more to the conflict between the Soviet Union and the West, in all likelihood, that conflict would not have issued in a cold war, but would have petered out, as did the conflict following World War I, in the willy-nilly accommodation of American idealism to the realities of the political world. The new dimension which set this conflict apart from its predecessor and transformed it into a cold war was the Communist character of the Soviet state and of its foreign policy. More particularly, it was Stalin's fusion of the traditional national interests of Russia with the tenets of communism and its misunderstanding by the West, as well as Stalin's misunderstanding of the West's reaction, that were responsible for that transformation.

To have transformed the tenets of communism into instruments for Russia's traditional foreign policy was the great innovative contribution Stalin made to the foreign policy of the Soviet Union. The nature of this contribution has been widely misunderstood. The Western world has looked upon Stalin as an orthodox Bolshevik, the fanatical proponent of a "rigid theology," [15] bent upon spreading the Communist gospel indiscriminately and by hook or crook to the four corners of the earth. Those who hold this view judge Stalin as though he were Trotsky: they confound Stalin's means, which comprise the classic Communist methods, ruthlessly applied, with his ends, which were in the tradition of Czarist expansionism rather than of Marxist-Leninist promotion of world revolution as an end in itself. Actually, in relation to Marxism-Leninism, Stalin's foreign policy was distinct from Lenin's and

---

[15] Arthur Schlesinger, Jr., in *New York Review of Books*, October 20, 1966, p. 37.

Trotsky's, on the one hand, and from that of Khrushchev and his successors, on the other.

Lenin saw in Russian bolshevism the doctrinal and political fountainhead of the Communist world revolution, and in the success of that revolution the precondition for the survival of the Bolshevist regime in Russia. Russian bolshevism was the "base" of world revolution; that was its historic function and justification in Marxist terms, as world revolution was Russian bolshevism's inevitable sequel and the guarantee of its success. On this doctrinal foundation, as developed in Lenin's *Left-wing Communism: An Infantile Disorder*, the Soviet Union stood in its earliest years as a guide and instigator of violent revolution throughout the world. Trotsky gave an extreme characterization to this first phase of Bolshevist foreign policy when he declared, on his appointment as People's Commissar for Foreign Affairs, "I will issue a few revolutionary proclamations to the people of the world and shut up shop." [16]

However, in contrast to Marx and the other Marxists, Lenin used Marxism not as a blueprint to be superimposed intact upon a recalcitrant reality but as an instrument for the acquisition of power. He reversed the priority between Marxism and power, traditional with the Marxists. One could say that he loved Marx, but he loved power more; he was a practitioner of power before he was an interpreter of Marx. Thus he decided what needed to be done for the sake of power, and then he used his version of Marx to justify what he was doing. One has only to read Lenin's polemics against Kautsky in order to realize how completely Marxism had changed its traditional function. Here we are no longer in the presence of a doctrinaire disputation in search of the Marxist truth for its own sake. Rather we are witnessing a phase in the conquest of power undertaken by a man with passionate fury who uses the doctrine as a hammer with which to obliterate views which, if accepted, might bar him from that conquest. What Lenin perfected for the domestic politics of the Soviet

---

[16] Quoted after E. H. Carr, *The Bolshevik Revolution, 1913–1923, III* (New York: The Macmillan Company, 1953), p. 16.

Union—the transformation of "the" science of society into an instrument for the acquisition of power—Stalin achieved for the foreign policies of the Soviet Union.

Both the consolidation of the Bolshevist regime within Russia and the collapse of the attempts at world revolution gave birth to Stalin's policy of "socialism in one country." Stalin's foreign policy in its first phase, lasting until victory in World War II, served the purpose of protecting the Soviet experiment from hostile outside intervention. During that period, Soviet foreign policy was haunted by the nightmare of a united front of the capitalistic powers seeking the destruction of the Soviet Union. The means Stalin employed to that end—clandestine military cooperation with Germany, temporary support of the League of Nations, the 1935 alliance with France, the implicit 1939 alliance with Germany—were in the classic tradition of power diplomacy. What was new was the additional power the Soviet Union could draw from its monolithic control of Communist parties throughout the world. The promotion of popular fronts and the Soviet intervention in the Spanish Civil War were the main manifestations of this new opportunity for the expansion of Soviet power.

How effective was this use of world communism for the purposes of the Russian state was strikingly revealed in the testimony of the British and Canadian members of the Grouzenko spy ring before the Royal Commission investigating the case. When asked why they had betrayed their own countries to the Soviet Union, almost all of these members replied that they had done it for the sake of humanity, that concern for humanity supersedes loyalty to any individual nation, and that the interests of humanity and those of the Soviet Union are identical. Communist internationalism and Russian nationalism are here brought into harmony. The Soviet Union appears endowed with a monopoly of truth and virtue, which sets it apart from, and above, all other nations. It may be pointed out in passing that here the Soviet Union is assigned the same privileged position among the nations which the proletariat occupies in Marxist philosophy among the classes.

From 1943 onwards, with Soviet victory over Germany assured, the main purpose of Soviet foreign policy changed from security to territorial expansion. Stalin sought to expand Soviet control primarily into territories adjacent to Russia, the traditional objectives of Russian expansionism. The conquest of Eastern Europe and of part of the Balkans, the pressure on Turkey for control of the Dardanelles and its northern provinces, the attempt to gain footholds on the Eastern shore of the Mediterranean and in northern Iran, the attempt to draw all of Germany into the Russian orbit, the recovery of the Russian interests in China—all these moves follow the lines of expansion tracked by the czars. The limits of Stalin's territorial ambition were the traditional limits of Russian expansionism. The former even fell short of the latter when political and military considerations appeared to make that retraction advisable. Thus Stalin honored the agreement with Great Britain of 1944, dividing the Balkans into spheres of influence; he recognized explicitly on the occasion of the Greek civil war that Greece was in the British sphere, and he lived up to that recognition in the policies he pursued. As Stalin said to Eden during World War II: "The trouble with Hitler is that he doesn't know where to stop. I know where to stop."

These traditional purposes of Stalin's foreign policy, as well as their misunderstanding by the West, are clearly and dramatically revealed in the confrontation at Yalta between Stalin and Roosevelt. From that confrontation, Stalin emerged as the power politician who, unencumbered by considerations of ideological advantage, sought to restore and expand Russia's traditional sphere of influence, while Roosevelt defended an abstract philosophic principle which was incapable of realization under the circumstances. Stalin could not help but interpret the Western position as implacable hostility to Russian interests, while the West saw in the ruthless transformation of the nations of Eastern Europe into Russian satellites empirical proof of the unlimited ambitions of Soviet communism.

This misunderstanding resulted from the combination of two factors: The actual communization of Eastern Europe and the attempted communization of much of the rest of Europe, and the use of Communist parties throughout the world on behalf of Soviet policies justified by Soviet spokesmen in terms of Marxism-Leninism. Thus by taking the Soviet government at its Marxist-Leninist word, one could not help concluding that Stalin was on his way to achieving what Lenin and Trotsky had been attempting in vain: To make the Marxist-Leninist prophecy of the communization of the world come true.

Haunted by the spectre of communism, Western opinion found it hard to appreciate the extent to which Stalin used Communist governments and parties as instruments for the ends of Russian power. He needed governments in Eastern Europe that were "friendly" to the Soviet Union. He did not care about the ideological character of these governments and parties so long as they were "friendly." Thus he tried to install aristocratic German generals in Germany and to come to terms with the Rumanian monarchy and a freely elected Hungarian government, and he failed. On the other hand, he established a stable *modus vivendi* with a non-Communist Finland. Yet he realized that, save for that exception, the only people in Eastern Europe who were willing to serve the interests of the Soviet Union were Communists. In private conversations, he heaped scorn upon the fools and knaves who allowed themselves to be used by him, but he used them because there was nobody else to use. And he was as hostile to Communist nationalists as he was to non-Communist ones. He purged the Communists of Eastern Europe who refused to do his bidding, for the same reason he was at best indifferent to Chinese communism, he exorcised and tried to bring down the Communist government of Yugoslavia, and he opposed the project of a federation of Communist Balkan states. For him, then, Communist orthodoxy was a means to an end, and the end was the power of the Russian state traditionally defined.

It is perhaps only in retrospect—by searching for the meaning of Stalin's policies in his private statements and kept commitments rather than in his public pronouncements, by comparing what Stalin did with what he could have done but did not do, and finally, by comparing Stalin's policies with those of his predecessors and successors—that one can assess correctly the nature of Stalin's foreign policy. And it is only in retrospect that one can savor the irony of the pope of Marxism-Leninism manipulating the tenets of the doctrine with cynical pragmatism on behalf of the national interests of Russia, while his Western opponents, more serious about the doctrine than he, sought the meaning of his deeds in the tenets of the doctrine.

## The Development of the Cold War

Thus the Cold War started. From then on, the issue was no longer whether spheres of influence should be abolished or maintained, but how far the sphere of influence of either side should extend. In the late 1940's Europe had for all practical purposes been firmly divided into two spheres of influence congealing into two military blocs, and the Cold War centered upon the concrete political issue of whether the line of military demarcation of 1945 dividing Germany was to be the definitive boundary between the two spheres, or whether the boundary ought to run farther east or west. That issue has remained unresolved to this day.

In that contest, the Soviet Union had two advantages: the Red Army was in physical possession of most of the territory the Soviet Union claimed to be its sphere of influence, and the Communist parties of Western Europe were at the beck and call of the Soviet government to support its policies. The West had nothing with which to oppose the Russian sphere of influence except legal and moral complaints about the violations of the Yalta agreements and the rhetoric of German unification, of "liberation" and "rollback." Against the extension of the Russian sphere it successfully used the weapons of military containment, the Marshall Plan, and the implementation of the Truman Doctrine.

The Cold War changed its character drastically under the impact of the hot war in Korea. The North Korean aggression was interpreted by the West as the opening shot in Moscow's campaign for the conquest of the world. It seemed to provide the clinching proof for the assumption held by the West since the beginning of the Cold War that Stalin's foreign policy was in line of succession not to the imperialism of the Tsars but to the worldwide Bolshevik aspirations of Lenin and Trotsky.

The misinterpretation of the North Korean aggression as part of a grand design at world conquest originating in and controlled by Moscow resulted in a drastic militarization of the Cold War in the form of a conventional and nuclear armaments race, the frantic search for alliances, and the establishment of military bases. This militarization was both the effect and the cause of the increased expectation that the Cold War might develop into a hot one. That expectation, shared by both sides, in turn increased the likelihood of such a development. As Mr. Halle wrote:

> By 1953 the entire foreign policy of the United States . . . was based on the Cold War. It made sense only on the premises on which the Cold War was being fought. Specifically, the policy was based upon the belief that Moscow was determined, by fraud or violence, to establish its ideology, its political system, and its domination over the entire world.

It is against this background that one must judge the import for the Cold War of Khrushchev's ascent to power. The view is widely held that Khrushchev was an improvement over Stalin in terms of the conduct of the Cold War; for Khrushchev is supposed to have sought the abatement of the Cold War through what he called "relaxation of tensions." I have never shared this view, and can only summarize here the arguments which I presented a decade ago in order to show that Khrushchev changed the quality and increased the range and the intensity of the Cold War but contributed nothing to its abatement. While Stalin conducted a Cold War of position, Khrushchev was the champion of a Cold War of movement. When Khrushchev spoke of relaxation of tensions, he wanted the West to stop challenging the *status quo* of 1945. In order to force the West to do this, he himself challenged the *status quo* of West Berlin at the risk of war. But in order to maintain the *status quo* of the Soviet empire he went to war in Hungary with methods as ruthless as any Stalin had ever used.

However, Khrushchev showed himself as the innovator of the Cold War of movement by making the whole world its theatre and by using new methods of waging it. Here he is the heir, not of Stalin and the Tsars, but indeed of Lenin and Trotsky. Khrushchev revived the Bolshevik expectation of the communization of the whole world as an immediate goal of Soviet foreign policy and made it the basis for a new policy which he called "competitive coexistence" tied to support for "wars of national liberation." His aims were the aims of Lenin and Trotsky, and the methods he used to achieve those aims were his original contribution to the Cold War. These methods run the whole gamut from military intervention and threats to diplomatic pressure, foreign aid and trade, support of subversion, and the exploitation of the new technological prestige of the Soviet Union. Thus, he threatened war with Great Britain and France over Suez and with the United States over Cuba. He competed with the United States and China for the allegiance of the new and emerging nations, and he transformed Cuba into a political and military outpost of the Soviet Union. This quantitative and qualitative transformation of the Cold War was the work of Khrushchev, not Stalin. It was Stalin, not Khrushchev, who said to Eden that the trouble with Hitler was that he didn't know where to stop. Khrushchev did not know it either, or he learned it only in 1962.

The post-Khrushchev phase of the Cold War is characterized by the extension of movement to the nations of Europe—East and West. In Europe, the aim of Khrushchev's Cold War of movement was identical with that of Stalin's Cold War of position—the stabilization of the political and territorial *status quo* of the immediate postwar period. In these two types of Cold War, two blocs opposed each other as political and military instruments of the two superpowers. Now the two tightly controlled blocs have been replaced by traditional alliances of varying closeness. Across the former boundary of the two blocs, whose impenetrable proximity was symbolized by the Iron Curtain, the nations of Eastern and Western Europe move in search of new alignments and configurations, putting into question not only the boundary but even the viability of the spheres of influence of the postwar period.

In the course of these movements, the natural weights of individual national powers have reasserted themselves. Thus, West Germany as the second most powerful nation on the European continent exerts a new attraction upon France, on the one hand, and upon countries like Czechoslovakia and Rumania, on the other. Do these developments spell the end of the Cold War? There is a tendency to answer that question in the affirmative, not in view of the relevant factors of interests and power in which the Cold War originated and which have kept it going for more than two decades, but in view of a superficial and obsolescent criterion—the degree of hostility exhibited by the United States and the Soviet Union in their relations with each other. From the fact that the United States and the Soviet Union have not challenged each other openly in recent years in Europe and the fact that their diplomatic relations are more nearly normal than they used to be, the conclusion can be drawn that there is nothing for them to fight about and therefore the Cold War has ended. However, the arms race continues and military bases remain intact. And the United States and the Soviet Union continue to oppose and compete with each other throughout the world. Vietnam and the Middle East are two spectacular cases in point. According to the *Economist* (November 19, 1966):

> The Middle East is one of the parts of the world where Cold War politics are far from dead; Russia and the West have their chosen protégés, and to preserve the balance keep them armed. The resultant arms race is something outsiders ought to get excited, as well as gloomy, about.

In Europe the conflict of interests that has pitted the United States against the Soviet Union since the end of World War II persists, even though it has taken on a new appearance. And the question which the Cold War brought to the fore two decades ago remains unanswered: Which way is Germany going to turn? Khrushchev saw clearly the crucial importance of that issue and expressed his confidence in a number of private conversations that sooner or later there would be "another Rapallo," that is, another alignment between the Soviet Union and Germany against the West.

This remains the crucial issue today as it has been for two decades, and it is a matter of secondary importance whether it is going to be fought out through the unilateral methods of the Cold War or through the traditional methods of diplomacy. The answer to that question depends primarily on the policies to be pursued by the Soviet Union. Thus far it has addressed West Germany in the Cold-War language of Stalin and Khrushchev. But how is it going to act? Will it try to protect the remnants of its empire against the attraction of West Germany through the unilateral methods of the Cold War? Or will it try to exchange what is left of that empire for a German-Soviet combination, which might promise to draw all of Europe into its orbit? Or will it use both methods simultaneously, or alternately, as the situation might suggest? Thus even if the Cold War should come to "an end"—and especially if it should—the diplomacy of the West (and, more particularly, of the United States) will have to deal with issues infinitely more complex, more risky, and also more promising than those it dealt with successfully during the first two periods of the Cold War. Until now, the West's main task has been to hold the line, and it has held it. It is an open question whether a less rigid Western diplomacy would have had a chance in 1953 and then again in 1956 to push that line farther east. In any event, from now on, the objective conditions of Europe rather than political rhetoric will pose the question as to where that line should be redrawn and whether there will be a line at all.

### Conclusions

Four conclusions follow from the foregoing analysis:

1. Both the orthodox and revisionist versions of the Cold War are untenable. It is as untenable to place all responsibility upon Stalin and communism as it is to put all the blame upon the American statesmen at the time and their hostility toward the Soviet

Union. However, revisionism has had the merit of reopening the issue of responsibility by questioning the orthodoxy of the forties and fifties.

2. The American opposition to an exclusive Soviet sphere of influence in Eastern Europe was not only quixotic, because it remained purely rhetorical since the United States had no intention of removing the Red Army from the countries of Eastern and Central Europe that it had conquered, but it was pernicious because it appeared to provide empirical proof for Stalin's suspicion of implacable Western hostility.

3. The worldwide aspirations of Soviet communism, either for their own sake or as means to the ends of Russian power, compelled the United States to view the expansion of the Soviet Union into Eastern and Central Europe not only in terms of the traditional national aspirations of Russia but also as worldwide aspirations of communism. Were these conquests self-sufficient means to the end of Russian security, or were they stepping stones on the road to world conquest? In all likelihood, the United States misunderstood Stalin's intentions, as Stalin misunderstood the intentions of the United States, each misunderstanding feeding upon the other.

4. As the Cold War originated in the impossibility of peace and the improbability of war, so the end of the Cold War is predicated upon the disappearance of one or the other of these factors. That is to say, the Cold War will come to an end either by escalating into a hot war or by the explicit or implicit settlement of the territorial issues remaining from World War II.

# Rejoinders

could control his Communist minions, suggests Professor Schlesinger, he could not control his own mental disorders. Yet, nowhere in the essay is there an attempt to reduce this generalization to specifics. In 1948 the Yugoslav Communist, Milovan Djilas, noted Stalin's mental decline since 1945, but made no such charge about Russian foreign policies since the end of the war. Professor Schlesinger himself gives us a political interpretation of specifics, stressing older Soviet (and Tsarist) efforts to create an Eastern European sphere of influence and new temptations to meddle in an unstable postwar Western Europe.

Stalin's behavior in the Iranian crisis of 1945–1946, to take but one example, was far from unbalanced, adventurist, or revolutionary, but revealed instead a calculated, cautious, and narrowly political initiative and response to a general American forward movement in the Middle East. Indeed, this crisis demonstrated more than anything else that the Soviet Union was unable to prevent the extension of American power and interests very nearly up to the Russian border itself without effective challenge. Russian influence in Iran was reduced as a result of this episode to perhaps its lowest point in the twentieth century.

In 1942, to take another example, FDR had invited the Soviets to take part in a trusteeship system over strategic areas of the world, but following Molotov's Yalta request for one of Italy's former African colonies, the United States reversed itself without concern for its own previous efforts to encourage Russian cooperation in the postwar security system. It is certainly not possible, in this instance, to sustain the argument that American officials based their policies upon Stalin's supposed irrationality.

That Stalin believed the capitalist world must *eventually* collapse, as an article of Marxist faith, probably was not so important to the origins of the Cold War as were American fears that Stalin believed the capitalist world must *soon* collapse, and was doing all that he could to speed up the process at every turn. President Truman was so convinced of this that he did not even wait for intelligence confirmations on the North Korean invasion of South Korea before deciding what the American response must be. As in other areas, Greece and China for example, Stalin's role in Korea has undergone reassessment in recent years. The last thing he wanted was a rearmed and unified West.

All three essays have a common beginning point: American universalism versus Soviet spheres of influence. Professor Schlesinger comments on each of the diverse factors that made up the American view, giving some attention to Cordell Hull's economic universalism. Of course I agree with that point, and would suggest further that Americans have believed for a long time that their economic expansion should not be considered on the same level with crasser geopolitical and territorial European imperialisms. This self-righteousness goes all the way back to Tom Paine's condemnation of the colonial connection with the British Empire (even while the colonists complained that London's moderate policies towards the Indians prevented their own expansionism), and has been a key part of America's traditional worldview and attitude toward old world politics, whether fashioned by a Tsar or commissar.

The argument that the Soviet Union was not a traditional nation-state in 1945 seems to me "a-historical," especially when it is expanded later to include the statement that nothing the United States could have done would have reduced Soviet intransigence and antipathy. What America *did do* in 1945 was to insist upon a unilateral interpretation of the Yalta Agreement (fully as much or more than the Soviets), and to engage in the bluntest form of economic pressure, while at the same time pushing the Russians to open up the Rhine-Danube region to Western economic influence. In this highly unstable situation, the United States dropped two atomic bombs on Japan. American motives in dropping those bombs are really not the issue; the effect was to increase East-West tensions in a variety of ways. Washington's representatives were careful not to rattle the bombs at the ensuing Foreign Ministers' Conferences, but even political cartoonists understood the situation, and often drew the bomb situated at the head of the peace table. To argue that Russia would have behaved in such-and-such a fashion regardless of what America did is to suppose an absolute rigidity in

Soviet policy and its reliance upon ideology, which falls down under any careful analysis of Russian behavior in this period.[1]

If Professor Schlesinger's treatment of American universalism is better and more comprehensive than Professor Morgenthau's, the latter's discussion of Roosevelt's reluctant and sporadic recognition that spheres of influence were not created by evil or disturbed men further substantiates the argument that Russian foreign policy after the war was neither ideologically nor psychologically determined. Professor Morgenthau isolates an important element in the origins of the Cold War: Stalin's use of the Communist Party apparatus. Even when it was used for conservative purposes, as in Italy where it was ordered to cooperate with Anglo-American efforts to create a rightist government, Stalin's apparent ability to manipulate such affairs was bound to alarm American leaders who had become responsible for world capitalism. Thus even if Italian Communists had been ordered to cooperate, those orders might someday be changed. Whatever the Kremlin intended, Stalin's use of the European Communist parties suggested to Americans that he had the power to employ them for his own devices. Even Russian domination of Eastern Europe through Communist control endangered American plans, not because its businessmen needed those markets, but because the American political-economic world system needed a revived Europe, and a revived Europe depended upon reestablished trade patterns. Ironically, the Russians tried to build a Communist economic system in Eastern Europe only after the United States put forward the Marshall Plan—in part to quiet complaints from their clients in those countries.

Professor Morgenthau tries to put Stalin's policies in perspective by comparing them to later Soviet activities outside of Europe. Nikita Khrushchev, he contends, advanced the Cold War from a struggle for position to a war of movement. Unlike Stalin, Khrushchev did not know where to stop—at least until 1962. The Soviet leader in these later days of the Cold War,

---

[1] See, for example, Marshall Shulman's excellent *Stalin's Foreign Policy Reappraised* (Cambridge: Harvard University Press, 1963).

he says, did not one thing to abate the struggle, despite the popular interpretation in the West that he was an improvement over Stalin. He suppressed the Hungarian revolution of 1956, threatened war with Britain and France over the Middle East and with the United States over Cuba. It is true that Russia's 1956 warning to the British and French over Suez challenged American hegemony in the Middle East, but the opportunity to take advantage of Arab nationalism was presented to the Kremlin by American blunders rather than by Communist conspiracy. Indeed, Khrushchev issued the warning only after it was clear that the United States and its allies were in disagreement; and it was an important means of diverting attention from the Hungarian situation, where Russian tanks were needed to suppress a nationalist uprising within the Soviet sphere. The United States promptly escalated its Middle Eastern policies with the "Eisenhower Doctrine." The Cuban issue is even less clear, moreover, and the notion that Russia had converted Cuba into a military outpost is refuted by Russian-Cuban disagreements over the prospects of Latin-American communism, and the techniques to be used in advancing the world revolution. In fact, Cubans complain the Russians would rather not encourage revolution in this area. In Professor Morgenthau's account, finally, Russian attempts to damp down the Cold War following Stalin's death—culminating in the 1955 Geneva Summit Conference—simply do not appear. It is odd that this should be so, since this is an area of his special expertise. However that may be, he prefers Stalin because the deceased dictator fit his theories better about "politics among nations."

Where all this leaves us is with a good measure of agreement on the essentials of the Russo-American clash at the outset of the Cold War, but with three different interpretations of the meaning of those essentials. America was at the pinnacle of its power and had the ability to determine, initially, the contours of the struggle. It would be interesting, in conclusion, to see how one would go about identifying the point where American Cold War policy lost control of the situation, or whether that was not inherent in its universalism from the beginning.

# 2

# Arthur Schlesinger, Jr.

$O$n reading
these three pieces, one is struck by the fact that, although there
are disagreements on peripheral questions and judgments, there is
a measure of convergence on two central propositions. All three
writers appear to conclude (a) that neither Moscow nor Washington was exclusively responsible for the Cold War, and (b) that
the Cold War resulted in great part from an almost inexorable
clash between two conceptions of international security—each
conception was held with great earnestness in one capital while
it was misconceived with equal earnestness in the other.

To assess the full significance of these central propositions,
however, one must have in mind the condition of the inter-

national power equilibrium in 1945. I think that all three essays, my own included, assumed too much that the authors should have stated explicitly; for the rise and decline of the Cold War cannot be understood without a recognition of the geopolitical dimension of world affairs—a dimension which played a role quite independent of ideology. World War II brought about a startling transformation in the structure of world power. The Axis states—Germany, Italy, Japan—were temporarily eliminated from the power equation. Most of the countries of Europe were militarily and economically exhausted. The European overseas empires were in process of disintegration. The ex-colonial world was in tumult and confusion. The war thus left in its wake a series of power vacuums around the planet.

It also left two states with the expansive energy—the political confidence and the military force—to fill these vacuums of power. In the decade after the end of World War II—the decade that came to an end with the conclusion of the war in Korea—the United States and Soviet Russia emerged as the first truly global powers in the history of man, exerting their influence everywhere around the earth, encountering no serious opposition anywhere, except from each other. The ideological discord between a capitalist democracy and a Communist dictatorship gave edge to the structural conflict. But, even without the ideological discord, the existence of the vacuums of power would no doubt have sucked these two dynamic states into competition and collision.

This structural predicament started the Cold War, as subsequent structural changes have reduced and diminished the Cold War. For the years since the end of the Korean War have seen the rise of a new force in revolt against the reign of the superpowers—or rather the resurgence of an older force latterly endowed with new potency and purpose. That force is nationalism —the determined quest on the part of smaller states for national identity and national freedom of decision. The rise of nationalism has meant growing opposition to the United States in the Western bloc, growing opposition to Soviet Russia in the Communist bloc, growing opposition to both America and Russia in the Third World, and growing boredom everywhere with the Russo-American Cold War. Nationalism, in short, has begun to place limits on the power of America and Russia. The age of the superpowers is plainly coming to an end; their best hope to protract their moment of dominance, indeed, is to move even faster toward a Russo-American alliance.

Or at least everyone sees this—except the superpowers themselves. A main source of trouble in the world today is, as often before, the failure of the superpowers to acknowledge an erosion of their capacity to command events. This is natural enough. Ordinarily it takes defeat in war to persuade a great power that it has been living beyond its means. Thus World War II took Italy and Japan out of the superpower game. Sometimes one defeat is not enough. It took two defeats, for example, to convince Germany that it was not a superpower; (there are those who fear that the Germans may not have learned the lesson yet). Britain and France, on the victorious side in World War II, persisted in the illusion until the defeat at Suez collapsed their imperial dreams. So America and Russia, propelled by the momentum of doctrines generated in the immediate postwar years, tend to cling, despite a new age and a changed world, to the habits of thought and action that worked more or less between 1945 and 1955.

The mirage of superpowership lay behind the American effort to decide the future of Vietnam, as it lay behind the Russian effort to nuclearize Cuba and to dominate the Middle East. Confronted by nationalism in the Dominican Republic, the United States had to use (or President Johnson thought it had to use) military force to maintain its sphere of influence in the Caribbean. Confronted by nationalism in Czechoslovakia, Russia had to use (or Kosygin and Brezhnev thought they had to use) military force to maintain its sphere of influence in Eastern Europe. Both powers got away in the short run with military interventions in their own spheres of influence; but even here they must both know that, when they are unwilling to use military force and accept political loss, they can no longer count on the automatic compliance of the countries of Eastern Europe or Latin America. And both failed miserably when they attempted intervention in more remote parts of the world—Vietnam or Cuba.

The American failure in Vietnam has produced a striking reassessment of the world position of the United States. President Kennedy had made the point in 1961, though his countrymen did not get around to accepting it until 1969:

> We must face the fact that the United States is neither omnipotent nor ominiscient—that we are only 6 per cent of the world's population—that we cannot impose our will upon the other 94 per cent—that we cannot right every wrong or reverse each adversity—and that therefore there cannot be an American solution to every world problem.

Vietnam has been an expensive and horrible education; but no one can question the fact that most Americans are now determined to have no more Vietnams. Bitter experience has thus compelled the Germans, the Japanese, the Italians, the British, the French, and recently the Americans to admit that they cannot live as superpowers in the age of nationalism. Only the Soviet Union, gripped by an increasingly anxious faith in the infallibility of its ideology, still seems to believe that there is a Soviet solution to every world problem, and this in spite of spectacular setbacks in Cuba and the Middle East. The world must hope that Czechoslovakia may in time have the same effect on Russia that Suez had on England and Vietnam on the United States.

This, I believe, is the background against which the Cold War must be viewed. As for the Cold War itself, my impression is that Professor Gardner in his interesting essay exaggerates the speed with which the United States responded to the alterations World War II wrought in the power equilibrium. If "the Western victors were haunted by the spectre of the Red Army marching into the chaos of Central Europe," we would hardly have had, for example, the extraordinary demobilization of the American Army in 1945. Also one misses, in Professor Gardner's account, any very vivid consideration of the mood and behavior of Soviet Russia. Did Stalin really do so little in these years to arouse legitimate apprehensions in the West?

Professor Gardner further implies on occasion, though he does not really argue the point, that the fundamental American motive was the "restoration of the capitalist world order"—that is, a determination to open all the world to American investment and American exports. He is not doctrinaire on this, though, and he is more accurate, I believe, when he writes, "Few American leaders seriously believed that East European markets and investments were worth all that fuss for any immediate benefit they might have to American postwar economic problems." In general, it may be said of most modern powers that political and strategic motives, including conceptions of the world order most conducive to national security, predominate over economic and commercial motives.

Moreover, the whole suggestion, in the spirit of William Appleman Williams, that a freely trading world is a bad thing, raises the question of alternative conceptions of international economic relationships. One may well believe that indiscriminate multilateralism is to the interest of the United States in the twentieth century, as it was to the interest of England in the nineteenth century, nor can anyone doubt that developing nations have a strong case for forms of economic protectionism. But, if a freely trading world is really so terrible as a long-term goal, should not those committed to the demonology of the Open Door state frankly a preference for bilateralism, economic nationalism, managed trading, or autarchy? Should they not at least provide us with a sketch of the economic arrangements they would deem so greatly preferable to those set forth, however imperfectly, at Bretton Woods?

I have the same sort of misgivings about the implications of Professor Morgenthau's trenchant piece. He too would seem to have an unstated alternative—in his case, a division of the world in 1945 based on a candid recognition of spheres of influence. America should not have contested Soviet hegemony in Eastern Europe, any more than Russia should contest American hegemony in the western hemisphere. Each superpower should be left free to cultivate its own garden.

But would it all really have been that easy? Professor Morgenthau misconstrues my reference to Stalin's "rigid theology." Of course I do not mistake Stalin for Trotsky or suppose that Stalin was dedicated to a program of world revolution. The phrase "rigid theology" referred not to Stalin's purposes but to his perception of American purposes—his belief that the mere existence of a capitalist state (or, indeed, as I argue in my piece, the existence even of a non-Stalinist Communist state) represented a mortal threat to the Soviet Union. This conviction, held firmly and even fanatically, would have made any sphere-of-influence deal inherently unstable, quite apart from the difficulty of getting the people of the West to accept the proposition that a war, begun to save Europe from one totalitarian dictator, should end by delivering half of Europe to another.

Had the West given Stalin a green light in Eastern Europe, he would have moved even more speedily and cruelly than he did to consolidate the Soviet position. Given his frame of mind and his absolute control over Soviet policy, the high probability is that the chaos of Western Europe in the years before the Marshall Plan would have been too tempting, and he would have used Eastern Europe as a springboard for further leaps to the West. As Harriman expressed an American view at the time, if a row were inevitable, better have it as far away as possible. (One should note, by the way, the extraordinary steadiness of Harriman's judgment through the years, especially since the revisionist historians tend to cast him as a villain in 1945. Actually his analysis of the Soviet problem changed in no essential respect in the quarter century after he became Ambassador to the Soviet Union; yet his recommendations responded sensitively to the changes in the international power equilibrium. This made him a "premature" advocate of containment in the forties and a "premature" advocate of negotiation in the sixties and, incidentally, won him a respect in the Soviet Union accorded to no other Western diplomat.)

As I do not quite grasp Professor Gardner's alternative to a freely trading world, neither do I quite grasp Professor Morgenthau's alternative to a system of world security. He eliminates Wilsonian universalism and seems to say that we must either have spheres of influence or world government: there is no middle way. I don't believe this for a moment. My guess is that any attempt to construct a world order on the basis of pure principle—whether of spheres of influence, or of universalism, or of world government—would be a great error.  The sphere-of-influence principle would inevitably lead to the oppression of small states, to the multiplication of Hungarys and Czechoslovakias in Europe and of Dominican Republics in Latin America.  In the present age of nationalism, it would involve the superpowers in a parade of police expeditions and military interventions.  On the other hand, the pure universalist principle would implicate the United States in Eastern Europe and the Soviet Union in Latin America in ways which the other side would interpret as genuinely threatening and which would vastly increase world tensions  The world government principle hardly seems worth consideration.

My belief is that realistic evolution in the future will be along the line of the proposal made by Churchill in 1943—that is, by blending the two principles of universalism and spheres of influence in a world organization that would give scope to both. A development of regional groupings and action *within* the United Nations, as permitted in Articles 52–54 of the Charter, would express the renewed force of nationalism, strengthen the middle powers, and discharge the great powers from rushing about to put down every presumed threat to world peace, or to themselves.  If the superpowers manage to divest themselves of their illusions, and if an international security system begins to base itself on the actualities of the contemporary power equilibrium, then we may hope at least to look forward to a time when the Cold War will really come to an end.

spanning the Pacific Ocean" and the fact that "policymakers in Washington decided upon war with Spain" appears to be far-fetched. It appears to be similarly far-fetched to interpret Russian expansion into the Far East as a parallel movement, conjuring up the prospect of a "contest for supremacy in Manchuria and China." If President Theodore Roosevelt was really "delighted" at the Japanese victory over Russia in 1904, he was not sufficiently delighted to allow the Japanese to establish their supremacy over Russia in the Far East; for he intervened in the peace negotiations on the side of Russia and justified his intervention with the American interest in the Asian balance of power. To link this with the Cold War as it developed out of World War II shows a historic imagination akin to science fiction rather than to empirical historiography.

The historical evidence does not support the assumption of a single-minded, purposeful American policy vis-à-vis Russia either at the turn of the century or at the end of World War II. Pursuing instinctively a balance-of-power policy in Asia, as it had in Europe since the beginning of the Republic, the United States was naturally glad to see Russia checked by Japan and vice versa. Similarly, when the Soviet Union emerged from World War II as the potentially hegemonial power on the European continent, the United States sought to contain it, as it had opposed Germany for the same reason in both World Wars.

Historical evidence is also lacking for Professor Gardner's statement that the atomic "bomb made it possible to take more risks . . . in dealing with Soviet-American political and economic conflicts." Which additional risks has Professor Gardner in mind? In truth, far from taking additional risks because it had the bomb, the United States was very careful to limit its risks exactly because it had the bomb. Berlin and Korea are cases in point, cited by Professor Gardner in support of his thesis. The American policymakers of the time were indeed aware of their ability to lay the Soviet Union waste with atomic bombs; but they were also aware of the likelihood that in case of war the Red Army would occupy Western Europe which would then have to be "liberated" with atomic bombs. That the monopoly of the atomic bomb increased the American sense of power stands to reason. But there is no historical evidence whatsoever for the revisionist proposition that the United States used this monopoly as a weapon in the Cold War against the Soviet Union. In the threats and promises of American diplomacy the monopoly of the atomic bomb played no role.

Professor Schlesinger shows convincingly how the traditional and, from the American point of view, rational confrontation between a potentially hegemonial Soviet Union and a United States, interested in the maintenance of and, if necessary, the restoration of the European balance of power, degenerated into the Cold War. Mutual misunderstandings generated a vicious circle of actions and reactions which were taken as empirical confirmations of the original false assumptions. He is less convincing in attributing the main responsibility for the tragedy to the ideological commitment of the Soviet Union and the character of Stalin. It would seem that a case could be made in favor of the proposition that the Western ideological commitment to the restoration of the pre-Fascist *status quo* and to anti-communism was much stronger and much less tempered by considerations of national interest than was the Russian commitment to the spread of communism. For the West, the ideological commitment was an end in itself; for the Soviet Union it was a means to the end of the security of the Russian state. More particularly, Stalin was not prevented by his psychological weaknesses from playing an extremely cynical and flexible game in Eastern Europe, becoming inflexibly committed to the imposition of communism only after it had become apparent that only Communist governments would do the bidding of the Soviet Union.

The United States was inflexibly committed not only to the restoration of the pre-Fascist *status quo* and to the opposition to communism, but also to the establishment of a "universal" world order as an alternative to traditional power politics. In enumerating the six reasons for this commitment to "universalism," Professor Schlesinger appears to be taking a favorable view of the commitment. I have always regarded this commitment as completely divorced from the reality of international relations and utterly quixotic in its application to Eastern Europe. It is possible to argue, as I have done, that the safety of Western Europe required us to contain the Russians as far east as possible. However, the time to do that was in 1944 and still at the beginning of 1945, when the Western allies devised their military strategy. Once we had allowed the Soviet armies to advance to a point one hundred miles east of the Rhine, the verbal attempts to roll them back were not only futile but pernicious, for they provided empirical proof for Stalin's suspicions.

B C D E F G H I J    5 4 3 2 1 7 0